My Mother Had a Dream

My Mother Had a Dream

THIS IS MY CHILD
SITTING IN THE SHADE,
HER HEAD THROWN BACK IN RAPTURE,
PROLONGING SOME MOMENT OF JOY
I HAVE CREATED FOR HER.
—Jamaica Kincaid

African-American Women Share Their Mothers' Words of Wisdom

Edited by
Tamara Nikuradse

A DUTTON BOOK

DUTTON
Published by the Penguin Group
Penguin Books USA Inc., 375 Hudson Street, New York, New York 10014, U.S.A.
Penguin Books Ltd, 27 Wrights Lane, London W8 5TZ, England
Penguin Books Australia Ltd, Ringwood, Victoria, Australia
Penguin Books Canada Ltd, 10 Alcorn Avenue, Toronto, Ontario, Canada M4V 3B2
Penguin Books (N.Z.) Ltd, 182–190 Wairau Road, Auckland 10, New Zealand

Penguin Books Ltd, Registered Offices: Harmondsworth, Middlesex, England

First published by Dutton, an imprint of Dutton Signet,
a division of Penguin Books USA Inc.
Distributed in Canada by McClelland & Stewart Inc.

First Printing, May, 1996
2   4   6   8   10   9   7   5   3   1

Page 254 constitutes an extension of this copyright page.

 REGISTERED TRADEMARK—MARCA REGISTRADA

LIBRARY OF CONGRESS CATALOGING-IN-PUBLICATION DATA:
My mother had a dream : African-American women share their
mothers' words of wisdom / edited by Tamara Nikuradse.
p.   cm.
ISBN 0-525-94111-8
1. Afro-American women—Life skills guides.   2. Afro-American women—Quotations.
3. Mothers and daughters—United States—Quotations.   I. Nikuradse, Tamara.
E185.86.M967   1996

305.48′896073—dc20

95-46897
CIP

Printed in the United States of America
Set in Matrix Book and Matrix Script
Designed by Eve L. Kirch

This book is printed on acid-free paper.

My Mother's Words of Wisdom

_____

_____

_____

_____

_____

_____

_____

_____

_____

_____

Turn this book into a keepsake by personalizing it with some of your mother's words of wisdom in the space provided above.

Contents

All good traits and learnings come from the mother's side.

—ZORA NEALE HURSTON

Introduction

Guided by my heritage of a love of beauty and a respect for strength—in search of my mother's garden,
I found my own.

—ALICE WALKER

My mother had a dream. . . .

More than thirty years ago, when my mother, Odeline
Cooper, left her home in the "backwoods" of Jamaica at sev-
enteen, she had a dream, a humble dream. But it was powerful enough to take her all the way to London. She vowed that
nothing was going to stop her from becoming a nurse and,
someday, living in the United States. An education in London
was the first step in what commenced a decade-long journey. Nourished by her courage, the dream fueled her
journey and inspired her to step foot on the freighter that
carried her across the ocean to England.

My mother had a dream. . . .

As it is with many journeys and many dreams, my mother
encountered a detour that forced her to reexamine her future. His name was Alexander Nikuradse, my father. When
they parted after my second birthday, she put the old
dreams away and looked to a new beginning, a new dream, a
dream for me.

If anyone cared to ask at this point, she said, "I have a dream for my daughter. . . ." Deferring her own dreams to give me a world of possibilities and opportunities, most of which she was denied, she shaped my dreams as surely as she had once woven her own.

She found a way to continue the journey, this time to Canada, after making provisions for me to stay with relatives in London at the age of two. I've only recently understood her courage and sacrifice and that there was no other way: she had to leave me behind as she forged ahead to prepare for my eventual arrival—and to insure my future.

She earned her nursing degree in Canada. She then made her way to the United States, settling down with a wonderful man, my stepfather, Charles Townes. She found work as a nurse. She'd accomplished her girlhood dreams, but now they were also the means of realizing her dream for her daughter.

By the time I reached nine years of age, my mother had saved enough money and was secure enough in her position to send for me. I followed the path she cleared. No goal seemed impossible. High school diploma. College degree. Graduate degree in medicine or law or business—or why not all three? Job. Job security. Advancement. Career. Family. She poured the concrete of my foundation with her example, her sweat, her sacrifice, her work ethic, her strong values, her sense of community, her charity, her common sense, her selflessness, her strong backbone, her faith in the Almighty, and her words of wisdom. . . .

Money doesn't grow on trees. Money's rooted in the soil. You have to till the earth, sow the seeds, raise the crop, and bloody your hands in the harvest. . . .

Honey, when it comes to men, keep your legs crossed, with one hand on the Bible and the other on your purse. . . .

Keep your two eyes open before you marry and one eye shut after you do. . . .

If you can read, you can do anything. . . .

Every time someone makes you mad, put some money in the bank. . . . You'll retire a millionaire!

In God we trust; all others pay cash. . . .

The Lord will provide. . . .

Lord have mercy. . . .

My mother had a dream. . . .
A dream that inspired her daughter to dream. . . .
A dream that anything was possible.

This book is a testimony to every mother clenching a dream for her daughter.

More than one hundred prominent African-American

women responded to the question, "What words of wisdom
or advice did your mother share with you to motivate, inspire, or help you realize your dreams?" Their original
responses are mixed with the public statements of many
other strong African-American women, past and present. (If
an excerpt doesn't give a "from" source, it is an original contribution to this volume.)

This collection is a chance for daughters to share the
dreams of their mothers and to explore how those dreams
became realities. Here are their words of wisdom and the
advice that motivated, inspired, or helped their daughters to
seize their own dreams.

Motherhood:
The Gift of Love

As little girls, one of our favorite games was playing house. We would play house for hours upon hours, reenacting the roles that swirled around in our real lives. The most coveted role in this make-believe world was that of mother. Although we all vied for this starring role, we realized that not just anyone could play mama. After much bickering, it was agreed that the girl with the most endearing traits should have the lead of mama, because it took someone with a big heart, warm, embracing arms, a loving smile, and a comforting voice to play this cherished role.

We put our mothers on pedestals, not so much out of respect, but out of simple admiration for them. Even as little girls, we understood that it took a very special person to be a mother. And it took an even better person to be a *good* mother: someone who would forsake everything she had for the good of her family, especially her children. If necessary, her dreams and hopes for herself were put on hold indefinitely so that she could help her little ones realize their dreams. She would forgo basic necessities so that her children would not be without, whether that meant saving the smallest portion for herself or wearing that same old dress and hat to church every Sunday for what seemed like an eternity. No matter how tired she was from work, she always found the energy to discipline us for our misdeeds or give us some extra sugar for our thoughtfulness. Whenever we felt down and out, mama was there to lift our spirits and make us feel oh, so special—even though many times it was *her* spirits that needed the lifting.

As we watch our daughters play house, let us hope that we can be at least half the mother to them that our mothers were to us. Let us hope that we can be their angels in disguise.

Hope and joy, peace and blessing
Met me in my firstborn child.

—FRANCES WATKINS HARPER, Founder of the
National Association of Colored Women
and author. From "The Mother's Blessing."

Mamas only do things cause they love you so much. They can't help it. It's flesh to flesh, blood to blood. No matter how old you get, how grown and on your own, your mama always loves you like a newborn.

—NTOZAKE SHANGE, daughter of Eloise Williams.
Author. From *Betsey Brown*.

Motherhood is a profession by itself, just like school teaching and lecturing.

> —IDA B. WELLS-BARNETT, daughter of Elizabeth Wells.
> Activist. From *Crusade for Justice*.

Oh, ye mothers, what a responsibility rests on you! You have souls committed to your charge, and God will require a strict account of you.

> —MARIA W. STEWART. Activist.
> From *Meditations from the
> Pen of Mrs. Maria W. Stewart*.

Stand by your own children, and suffer with them till death. Nobody respects a mother who forsakes her children.

> —HARRIET A. JACOBS, daughter of Delilah Horniblow.
> Activist. From *Incidents in the Life of a Slave Girl*.

The currents that flow between Black mothers and their daughters are often tumultuous, deepened and intensified by the racism and sexism of White America. Black mothers, particularly those with strong ties to their community, sometimes build high banks around their young daughters, isolating them from the dangers of the larger world until they are old enough and strong enough to function as autonomous women. Often these dikes are religious, but sometimes they are built with education, family, or the restrictions of a close-knit and homogeneous community. Even when relieved by eddies of tenderness, this isolation causes the currents between Black mothers and daughters to run deep and the relationship to be fraught with an emotional intensity often missing from the lives of women with more freedom.

—ROSALIE RIEGLE TROESTER. Author. From "Turbulence and Tenderness," *Double Stitch*.

Woman, Mother—your responsibility is one that might make angels tremble and fear to take hold!

> —ANNA JULIA COOPER, daughter of Hannah Stanley.
> Activist and educator. From *A Voice from the South*.

Africa is herself a mother. The mother of mankind. We Africans take motherhood as the most sacred condition human beings can achieve.

> —MAYA ANGELOU, daughter of Vivian Baxter. Educator and author.
> From *My Soul Looks Back, 'Less I Forget*.

Children are a blessing from God—blessings come with many responsibilities.

> —BRENDA J. LAUDERBACK, daughter of Dorothy Lauderback.
> Group president, Nine West Group, Inc.

I think black women, whether they were strong women or whether they were beaten and broken down, had a belief in the goodness of the future. They always wanted another world that would be better for their children than it had been for them. The black woman has deep wells of spiritual strength. She doesn't know how she's going to feed her family in the morning, but she prays and in the morning, out of thin air, she makes breakfast.

—MARGARET WALKER, daughter of Marion Dozier Walker.
Poet and educator. From *I Dream a World*.

Everything I have learned about love, I learned from my mother. For it is mothers who bend, twist, flex, and break most dramatically before our uninitiated eyes. Fathers bear, conceal, inflict, sometimes vanish, so the mythology of domestic union tells us. But mothers absorb, accept, give in, all to tutor daughters in the syntax, the grammar of yearning and love.

—MARITA GOLDEN, daughter of Beatrice Lee Reid.
Author. From *Wild Women Don't Wear No Blues*.

I had grown big, but my mother was bigger, and that would always be so.

—JAMAICA KINCAID, daughter of Annie Richardson.
Author. From "My Mother."

*I'll be with you always, and even when you
don't want me to be.*

—DIANA ROSS, daughter of Ernestine Ross. Entertainer.
From *The Mother Book*.

Roots: The Gift of Heritage

As we look at all the strong African-American women who are reaching new heights of success and breaking what once seemed like concrete barriers, we must never forget the struggles of our foremothers, who blazed the trails before us.

We are strong, powerful women today because of the sacrifices these women made in order to provide a better world for their children, grandchildren, and great-grandchildren to live in. Let us not forget the matriarchs. Women who carried their babies on their backs as they labored under the intense sun picking cotton. Women who cleaned and cooked for another family only to have to do it all over again at the end of the day in their homes. Women who stood their ground against ferocious dogs, powerful fire hoses, and the hostile grins of bigots, all in the name of equality. Women who worked from sunup till sundown in the dingy, muggy textile mills, spinning cloth for thankless strangers. Women who refused to submit to the intoxications of poverty because they wanted to nourish their children with pride. Women who never lost faith in the Almighty even though others had. Let us not forget, their blood, sweat, and tears made us who we are today—they are our backbone, a backbone strong enough to carry our nation.

She always talked about roots, about values that were anchored in loving yourself, but also in loving your people. Your roots. "Little people make big people," she would say, "and big people become small people when they forget where they came from."

—GLORIA WADE-GAYLES, daughter of Bertha Wade.
Author. From "Connected to Mama's Spirit,"
Double Stitch.

*We are African women and we know, in our
blood's telling, the tenderness with which
our foremothers held each other.*

—AUDRE LORDE, daughter of Linda Belmar Lorde.
Author. From "Eye to Eye."

I think I see her sitting bowed and black,
    Stricken and seared with slavery's mortal scars,
Reft of her children, lonely, anguished yet
    Still looking at the stars.

> —JESSIE REDMON FAUSET, daughter of Annie Seamon.
> Author. From "Oriflamme."

My grandmothers were strong.
They followed plows and bent to toil.
They moved through fields sowing seeds.
They touched earth and grain grew.
They were full of sturdiness and singing.
My grandmothers were strong.
My grandmothers are full of memories . . .

> —MARGARET WALKER, daughter of Marion Dozier Walker.
> Author. From "Lineage."

My mother first took us south to visit her Tennessee birth-place one summer when I was seven or eight. I woke up on the backseat of the car while we were still driving through . . . Kentucky and my mother was pointing out the beautiful hills and telling my brothers about how her father had run away and hidden from his master in those very hills when he was a little boy. She said that his mother had wandered among the wooded slopes in the moonlight and left food for him in secret places. They were very beautiful hills and I looked out at them for miles and miles after that, wondering who and what a "master" might be.

—LORRAINE HANSBERRY, daughter of Nannie Perry Hansberry.
Playwright. From *To Be Young, Gifted and Black.*

If I saw young girls from their mothers' arms,
Bartered and sold for their youthful charms,
My eye would flash with mournful flame,
My death-paled cheek grow red with shame.

—FRANCES ELLEN WATKINS HARPER. Activist.
From "Bury Me in a Free Land."

I am my mother's daughter and the drums of Africa still beat in my heart. They will not let me rest while there is a single Negro boy or girl without a chance to prove his worth.

—MARY McLEOD BETHUNE, daughter of
Patsy McIntosh McLeod.
Activist and educator.
From "Faith That Moved a Dump Heap."

I didn't have a soap-opera view of life. . . . I grew up know-ing it wasn't going to be easy, but my mother called great women to my attention—women like Marian Anderson and Lena Horne.

> —DOLORES CROSS, daughter of Ozie Johnson Tucker.
> President, Chicago State University. From *Essence*, April 1992.

My consciousness of the world beyond the family developed on two planes—"the race of colored people" and "the white people." My aunts were "race women" of their time. They took pride in every achievement of "the race" and agonized over every lynching, every black boy convicted and "sent to the roads," every insult to "the race." I would hear: "The race is moving forward!" "You simply can't keep the race down!" "The race of colored people is going to show the world yet!"

> —PAULI MURRAY, daughter of Agnes Georgianna
> Fitzgerald Murray. Activist, lawyer, minister.
> From *Song in a Weary Throat*.

I have ploughed, and planted, and gathered into barns, and no man could head me—and ain't I a woman? I could work as much and eat as much as a man—when I could get it—and bear the lash as well! And ain't I a woman? I have borne thirteen children and seen 'em mos' all sold off to slavery, and when I cried out with a mother's grief, none but Jesus heard me! And ain't I a woman?

—SOJOURNER TRUTH, daughter of Elizabeth
Mau-Mau Bett Baumfree. Activist. From her
address "And ain't I a woman?"

Mother was of royal African blood, of a tribe ruled by matriarchs. . . . Throughout all her bitter years of slavery she had managed to preserve a queenlike dignity.

—MARY McLEOD BETHUNE, daughter of Patsy McIntosh McLeod.
Activist and educator. From "Faith That Moved a Dump Heap."

Only the *black woman* can say "when and where I enter, in the quiet, undisputed dignity of my womanhood, without violence and without suing or special patronage, then and there the whole *Negro race enters with me.*"

—ANNA JULIA COOPER, daughter of Hannah Stanley.
Activist and educator. From *A Voice from the South.*

My great-grandmama told my grandmama the part she lived through that my grandmama didn't live through and my grandmama told my mama what they both lived through and my mama told me what they all lived through and we suppose to pass it down like that from generation to generation so we'd never forget.

—GAYL JONES, daughter of Lucille Jones.
Author. From *Corregidora.*

To be a woman of the Negro race in America, and to be able to grasp the deep significance of the possibilities of the crisis, is to have a heritage, it seems to me, unique in the ages.

—ANNA JULIA COOPER, daughter of Hannah Stanley.
Activist and educator. From *A Voice from the South.*

My own momma done better than she could and my momma's momma, she done better than she could. And everybody's momma done better than anybody had any right to expect she would. And that's the truth!

—JUNE JORDAN, daughter of Mildred Maud Fisher Jordan. Activist, author, and professor. From her address at Williams College: "Don't You Talk About My Momma!"

Unlike "Ma" Rainey's songs, which retained their creator's name even while blasting forth from Bessie Smith's mouth, no song or poem will bear my mother's name. Yet so many of the stories that I write, that we all write, are my mother's stories. Only recently did I fully realize this: that through

years of listening to my mother's stories of life, I have ab-
sorbed not only the stories themselves but something of the
manner in which she spoke, something of the urgency that
involves the knowledge that her stories—like her life—must
be recorded.

> —ALICE WALKER, daughter of Minnie Tallulah Grant Walker.
> Author. From "In Search of Our Mothers' Gardens."

I have taken all of my children to Africa, and now I've
started taking grandchildren. But it's not a trend or a fad for
us. It's an aspect of personality development that is firm and
fixed and essential. . . . Until we as Afro-Americans are fully
rejoined with Africa, in terms of pride and knowledge of our
ancestry, we will never be whole people.

> —RACHEL ROBINSON, mother of Jackie, Jr., David,
> and Sharon Robinson. Chairperson of the Jackie Robinson
> Foundation. From *I Dream a World.*

The mother is there to protect you.
She is buried in Africa,
and Africa is buried in her.
That is why she is supreme.

—CAMARA LAY. Author. From *The Dark Child.*

[My grandmother is] an ancestor figure—African and New World—who made my being possible and whose spirit I believe continues to animate my life and work. I am, in a word, an unabashed ancestor worshiper.

—PAULE MARSHALL, daughter of Ada Clement Burke.
Author. From *African-American Woman Quote Book.*

Bringing the gifts that my ancestors gave,
I am the dream and the hope of the slave.
I rise
I rise
I rise.

—MAYA ANGELOU, daughter of Vivian Baxter.
Educator and author. From "Still I Rise."

Readin', Writin', 'Rithmetic: The Gift of Learning

"If you can read, you can do anything." How many times did we hear these words as we were growing up? Or how many times in a day did our mothers reply, "I'm not a walking encyclopedia. Go look the answer up," when we belabored them with one of our incessant questions? If the answer couldn't be found in our tattered, secondhand encyclopedia, surely it could be found in the library.

How fondly I remember the Saturday afternoons that I'd spend in the public library finding all the answers to the umpteen questions I didn't have answers to. The library was a magical place that seemed to contain answers to all life's mysteries.

My mother always encouraged my pursuit of learning in other ways as well. There were no toys at Christmastime for Tamara, only books and clothes—"the real necessities of life." Even though we lived from paycheck to paycheck throughout my childhood, my mother was always able to scrape together a few dollars so I could pay dues for Girl Scouts or Junior Achievement. She went without a new pair of shoes for work to be able to buy me a dictionary or send me to a learning camp.

At the time, I had no idea that she was instilling in me a high regard for education. In her quiet way, she made me want to pursue an education. I truly came to believe my mother's words of wisdom that "if you can read, you can do anything!"

Mothers are the levers which move in education. The men talk about it . . . but the women work most for it.

—FRANCES ELLEN WATKINS HARPER. Activist.
From "The Coloured Women of America."

Knowledge is the prime need of the hour.

—MARY McLEOD BETHUNE, daughter of Patsy McIntosh McLeod.
Activist and educator. From *Ebony*, 1955.

At an early age my mother sowed the idea of a doctorate in my fertile mind. Although at the time neither of us knew that such a degree existed, she constantly stressed that I had to get as much education as possible because when she was growing up in the rural south most blacks were not even allowed to attend school. And so it was up to me to take advantage of every educational opportunity. As I neared forty, despite the fact that I had long dreamed of obtaining my degree, I had many excuses as to why I couldn't go to school. In the midst of my complaints about being too old, too weary, and too poor, my Mama Dear sat silently and listened. She did not argue my rationalizations with me, but in her wisdom replied, "You are going to be all of those things anyway. You might as well be them with letters behind your name." As ever, the truth and simplicity of her words, which have always sustained me, rang out louder and clearer than my demons of self-doubt and pity.

—JUANITA JOHNSON-BAILEY, Ed.D., daughter of Georgia Mae Johnson. Professor, University of Georgia.

Mother saw to it that we were in earnest about our schooling. She has always had a way of saying things that I feel are things to live by. About school tasks at home, she said, "If it takes you half an hour to do your lessons and it takes someone else fifteen minutes, take the half hour and do them right." It took me some time to realize the value of this advice and what it implied. If we can't do a thing as quickly as someone else, then take the necessary time and do a good job.

—MARIAN ANDERSON, daughter of Annie Anderson. Opera diva. From her autobiography, *My Lord, What a Morning.*

I understood education before I understood anything else. From the time I was two, my mother said, "You will go to college. Education is your key to survival," and I understood that.

—MELBA PATTILLO BEALS. Activist and one of the nine children to desegregate Central High School in Little Rock in 1957. From *Voices of Freedom*.

Get a good education because knowledge is power, and once you have it, no one can take it away.

—ANITA DOREEN DIGGS, daughter of Gladys Haigler-Smith. Author of *Talking Drums* and *Success at Work*.

My mother read poetry to me before I could read, and I can't remember when I couldn't read. We grew up with books. I don't think you can write if you don't read. You can't read if you can't think. Thinking, reading, and writing all go together. When I was about eight, I decided that the most wonderful thing, next to a human being, was a book.

> —MARGARET WALKER, daughter of Marion Dozier
> Walker. Poet and educator. From *I Dream a World*.

I feel certain I would not be a published writer if my mother had not told me the following: "Read. Read well and read to understand. If you can read, you can do anything, because what others have created or accomplished has been written about. If you go to the library, you will find information to inspire you and guide you to accomplish *anything* you want to do."

I took her words to heart and still do. Whenever I am starting a project, the first place I go is the library. What a wonderful place it is!

> —ANITA R. BUNKLEY, daughter of Virginia L. Richmond.
> Author of the African-American historical novels
> *Black Gold*, *Wild Embers*, and *Starlight Passage*.

Jeanne Terborg, my mother, is in the tradition of generations of African-American women who have passed their
mothers' words of wisdom to their daughters. Time and time
again when I was growing up, she said what her mother had
said to her: "Pretty is as pretty does." Doing nice things for
people, Jeanne said, being kind to people, being respectful
and acting like a "lady," were what made you a "pretty" person. So she advised me, as I advise my daughter, not to be
impressed only with the way you and others look and the
clothes you and they wear. Do "pretty" things and search for
friends who are "pretty" because of the things they do.

When in the 1960s I was graduating from college, with
trepidation about going to graduate school, my mother encouraged me to go on with my education. She told me to be
prepared so that I could be independent enough to take care
of myself, just in case my future husband could not. Although she had been fortunate enough to find a husband
who enabled her to stay home with his children while we
grew up, she said I may not be so lucky. Jeanne reminded
me that she and both of my grandmothers had skills that
allowed them to provide important income to their house-
holds. Furthermore, she assured me that both of my grandmothers had encouraged her to be financially prepared for
any circumstance. For my generation even more than hers,
my mother believed that advanced education was the key.

She also knew that becoming a professional was not enough, because "pretty is as pretty does."

> —DR. ROSALYN TERBORG-PENN, daughter of
> Jeanne Van Horn Terborg. Professor at Morgan
> State University and editor of *Black Women in
> America: An Historical Encyclopedia*.

Women are the first teachers, so they should always get an education.

—KARA YOUNG, daughter of Rosemarie Young. Fashion model.

My mother always told me to be overqualified for everything. She said, "Always have more qualifications than anybody else you're sitting in the room with. If there are people there who have one degree, you get two. If they got two, you get three."

> —MARY FRANCES BERRY, daughter of Frances Southall Berry.
> Historian, educator, attorney, activist, and government
> official. From *I Dream a World*.

I tell my children, Never use the words *I can't*. Say *I'll try*. I tell them, "Now God has given us something up in the head, and you know why He put it there? Because He wants you to use it. If you don't use it, He is going to take it away and give it to the next boy or girl."

When they bring their big bags to school, I say, "Leave your pocketbook at home." I say, "When you fill up your head, then the head will help you to fill up your pocketbook."

—RUBY MIDDLETON FORSYTHE, daughter of Marthenia E. Middleton.
Teacher for over 60 years in South Carolina. From *I Dream a World*.

My mother viewed speaking impeccably proper English as a strategy in the overall battle for civil rights.

—BEBE MOORE CAMPBELL, daughter of Doris Moore.
Author. From *African-American Woman Quote Book*.

My mother was not one to offer words of wisdom. Instead, she led by example. She was curious about everything—the mundane to the profound. For her, all experiences were learning opportunities. My mother often read what I was reading, from Dr. Seuss to Friedrich Nietzsche. Then, we would have full-blown debates about *ideas*. She would often thank me for teaching her something new. In short, my mother always took me seriously. She simply assumed I would be successful in whatever I did.

—LINDA A. HILL, daughter of Lillian Virginia Gordon Hill.
First African-American woman to receive tenure at
the Harvard Business School and the author of
Becoming A Manager: Mastery of a New Identity.

I told them what I tell them now . . . always seek new knowledge . . . there must always be some kind of program, some new study, some challenges to jack the mind up and make it use some of the cells it hasn't used before.

—VIVIAN ALLEN AYERS, mother of Phylicia Rashad
and Debbie Allen. Pulitzer Prize–nominated author.
From *Ebony*, February 1988.

*Education remains the key to both economic
and political empowerment.*

—BARBARA JORDAN, daughter of Arlyne Patten Jordan.
Educator and former congresswoman.
From *Words to Make My Dream Children Live*.

My mother was a great advocate of education. She was not able to provide financial support for college, but she gave me unlimited moral support. She always told me that I could be whatever I wanted to be if I had the confidence and was willing to work for what I want.

—LILLIAN LINCOLN, daughter of Arnetha Hobson.
President, Centennial One, and first African-American
woman to graduate from the Harvard Business School.

"You, Mary Frances! You're smart. . . . You can think, you can do all the things I would have done if it had been possible for me. . . . You have a responsibility to use your mind and to go as far as it will take you."

—MARY FRANCES BERRY, daughter of Frances
Southall Berry. Historian, educator, attorney,
activist, and government official.
From *Ms. Magazine*, January 1987.

Identity: The Gift of Self

Our mothers had a defiance about them when it came to raising us. No one was going to tell them how to raise their daughters. They insisted that we learn the hard knocks of life early on.

As a child growing up in Cheektowaga, New York, I always thought that all the black mothers were *real* tough. Not only tough to strangers, but tough with their own children. While my white friends got to run around after school, it seemed as if my black girlfriends and I had to go straight home to a world of chores, homework, and baby-sitting. While other kids got rewarded with hugs and kisses for getting B's on their report cards, we were sternly asked, "Why didn't you get an A?"

How I longed with my girlhood friends, Marcia and Cheryl, to have carefree childhoods where we were free to do as we pleased. When we mercilessly complained to each of our mothers about how hard our lives were compared to those of many of our white friends, without skipping a beat they gave the identical retort, "I don't care what everyone else is doing!" We would come to hear this answer over and over again, no matter what the question.

Unfortunately, as children we could not grasp the long journey that our mothers were preparing us for by nurturing us on tough love. We had to be strong and independent. It was simply unacceptable to flow with the crowd or be like the others. Although our mothers did not use the same words as writer Gloria Wade-Gayles's mother, the message was the same: "Phony things can mess up your values. . . . If you start trying to be like other people because of who they are, or who you think they are . . . you'll end up not being yourself."

"Look at'cha. You's a pretty black gal!"

—ALFRE WOODARD, daughter of
Constance Roberson Woodard. Actor.

I still hear you humming, Mama. The color of your song calls me home. The color of your words saying, "Let her be. She got a right to be different. She gonna stumble on herself one of these days. Just let the child be." And I be, Mama.

—SONIA SANCHEZ, daughter of Lena Jones Driver.
Author. From "Dear Mama," in *Under a Soprano Sky*.

My mother shared *many* words of wisdom with me. However, the advice she gave that had the most impact was this: "Sleep with your own eyes." That simple phrase was her way of saying do not depend on anyone, and if there is something that you want, set your goal, work hard, and achieve it on your own.

—KATE FERGUSON, daughter of Mary Ferguson.
Editor in chief, *Today's Black Woman*.

"Child, go look at yourself in the mirror." It was always said as if whatever I saw surpassed good and bordered on the truly wonderful. And I, searching for my own reflection, walked away oblivious to the love and life-sustaining messages which had seeped into my pores as I sat on the floor of my mother's kitchen.

—WILLI COLEMAN, daughter of Nettie Coleman. Author. From "Closets and Keepsakes," *Double Stitch*.

Being different in any way isn't easy, but for my mother being a leader, or standing alone, is always better than being part of the crowd, especially the wrong crowd. "I don't care what everyone else is doing. You're not everyone else's child; you're *my* child." To this day I live her words and thank her in my heart constantly.

—LAVADA B. NAHON, daughter of Roxie D. Blanton. Senior editor, *Penthouse*.

Phony things can mess up your values. . . . If you start trying to be like other people because of who they are, or who you think they are, . . . you'll end up not being yourself.

—GLORIA WADE-GAYLES, daughter of Bertha Wade. Author. From "Connected to Mama's Spirit," *Double Stitch.*

It's because of my mother, Gloria—a beauty in her own right, dark skinned, fine featured, so proper, such a lady—that I've learned so much about the meaning of true beauty, inside and out. Like so many women, I vividly remember watching my mother get dressed to go out—painstakingly putting on her makeup, adjusting the tilt of her hat, slipping on feminine, high-heeled shoes. She had, and still has, a way about her—a love of beauty and quality—that I know influenced me greatly. And her innate sense of elegance still manages to make the simplest things she wears look special . . . and beautiful.

—BEVERLY JOHNSON, daughter of Gloria Johnson. Fashion model. From *True Beauty.*

When I was a girl, my mom would always tell me, "Jayne, in this life you are never going to be able to please everyone, so you must conduct your life in a way that pleases yourself." Well, when you're young it sounds corny, and for a long time I didn't really understand the importance of what Mom was saying. But as I got older and made many mistakes, I came to realize how right she was. In the past I always tried so hard to please other people, to be what *they* wanted me to be, instead of just who I am.

> —JAYNE KENNEDY-OVERTON, daughter of
> Virginia Harrison. Actor. From *Ebony*,
> February 1988.

I saw a lot of the young me in *Queen*. . . . The confusion, the uncertainty, not really knowing if you should be black or white. . . . My mother cleared it up for me when I was very young. . . . She said when you look in the mirror you're going to see a black woman. You're going to be discriminated against as a black woman, so ultimately, in this society, that's who you will be. And that's made my life very easy. . . . I think if you're an interracial child and you're strong enough to live "I'm neither black nor white but in the middle," then, more power. But I *needed* to make a choice and feel part of this culture. I feel a lot of pride in being a black woman.

—HALLE BERRY, daughter of Judith Berry.
Actor. From *Ebony*, April 1993.

In high school, I was intimidated because everyone saw me as "Marva's child." I hated school. I wanted to change schools, but she said that wasn't the answer. I will always be who I am, and I can't just turn my back and walk away from it. Everybody said she was crazy to leave her job and start the school. She just ignored them, and now look at how many lives she's touched. That taught me that it's not what you have, but what you make of it.

—CYNTHIA COLLINS, daughter of Marva Collins.
Educator. From *Ebony*, May 1989.

You are ultimately responsible for you. You must not expect anyone else to take care of you. If they do, fine, but don't rely on anyone else other than you and God for your self-survival. Never let anyone take your independence away.

—KATHY RUSSELL, daughter of Dorothy Clarese Russell.
Author of *The Color Complex: The Politics of Skincolor
Among African-Americans* and *Divided Sisters:
Bridging the Gap between Black Women
and White Women.*

*"Don't ever depend on connections, baby. . . .
That's like depending on somebody else.
Connect to yourself."*

—GLORIA WADE-GAYLES, daughter of Bertha Wade. Author.
From "Connected to Mama's Spirit," *Double Stitch.*

My grandmother, who was one of the greatest human beings I've ever known, used to say, "I am a child of God and I'm nobody's creature." That to me defined the black woman through the centuries.

—MAYA ANGELOU, granddaughter of Annie
Henderson. Educator and author.
From *Essence*, December 1992.

Fundamentals:
The Gift of Values

Our mothers grounded us in the fundamentals of life by instilling values in us that made us law-abiding, God-fearing, family-loving people. Our mothers—our moral compasses, our role models—taught us to be honest, hardworking daughters who always extended a hand to help others in need even if that meant we had to do without. Little did we know that by helping others we would come to see how truly blessed and loved we were despite the few possessions that we had.

They taught us to respect others. They taught us to speak the truth. They taught us the meaning of sacrifice. They instilled in us the hurdle of a moral high ground and challenged us to jump higher. They taught us how to be good friends. They taught us how to love. They taught us the act of charity. They taught us to follow our hearts. They taught us to do what we thought was the right thing to do, because we had three people to answer to: ourselves, our mother, and the Lord. They taught us the meaning of the word *values* through the example of their own daily lives.

I just want you to remember one thing. From the moment you leave this house, don't let anybody raise you. Every time you get into a relationship you will have to make concessions, compromises, and there's nothing wrong with that. But keep in mind Grandmother Henderson in Arkansas and I have given you every law you need to live by. Follow what's right. You've been raised.

—MAYA ANGELOU, daughter of Vivian Baxter.
Educator and author. From *Double Stitch*.

Daughter, as you go about fulfilling your dreams
Stand up for the good and fight the good fight
Laugh long, always follow your right mind
And sleep gentle at night.

—JOYCE CAROL THOMAS, daughter of Leona Haynes.
Author and winner of the National Book Award
for her novel *Marked by Fire*.

Never get tired of doing the right thing.

—DELORES SPRUELL JACKSON, daughter of Mamie Spruell.
Producer of *Live with Regis and Kathie Lee*.

Charity begins at home, and then spreads abroad.

> —SUSAN L. TAYLOR, daughter of Violet Weekes
> Taylor. Editor in chief, *Essence,* and author of
> *In the Spirit* and *Lessons in Living.*

Mama didn't offer a lot of advice, she didn't even talk about God, but she showered love and a hot meal and even a sofa to sleep on to anyone who was in need. She worked hard, played cards, bet on the horses, drank Ole Grand Dad, and went to church some Sundays. She had lots of friends, and I remember her saying to me: "Jeannie, the best thing in the world is a good friend. But you gotta be a good friend to have a good friend." I am a very wealthy woman—I have lots of good friends today, thanks to Mama's advice.

> —REGINA NICKERSON JONES, daughter of Luedelia Nickerson.
> Poet, publicist, and owner, Regina Jones & Associates.

The true worth of a race must be measured
by the character of its womanhood.

> —MARY McLEOD BETHUNE, daughter of Patsy McIntosh McLeod.
> Activist and educator. From "A Century of Progress
> of Negro Women."

We were to become young ladies—poised, modest, accomplished, educated, and graceful, prepared to take our places in the world.

> —SHIRLEY CHISHOLM, daughter of Ruby Seale St. Hill. Former congresswoman and first woman to run for president of the United States. From *Epic Lives*.

Many times you are a role model for people you don't even know—live your life accordingly.

> —BRENDA J. LAUDERBACK, daughter of Dorothy Lauderback. Group president, Nine West Group, Inc.

My mother taught me that the most important things in life are not visible to the naked eye. Those things are in the mind and heart. . . . Being true to myself . . . and the commitment to my work.

—TYRA FERRELL, daughter of Rachel Johnson.
Actor. From *Essence*, July 1992.

When I was a child, she often said, "Mommy always wants you to remember this one thing: To thine own self be true," and that always stuck with me. And she'd say, "You'll understand it better as you go through life," and she's so right. It is so important.

—WHITNEY HOUSTON, daughter of Cissy Houston.
Entertainer. From *Ebony*, January 1993.

Bread cast upon the waters comes back one thousand fold.
Give out good, and good comes back to you.
Give out evil, and evil comes back to you.
Everything that goes around, comes around.

—DR. MARGARET T. G. BURROUGHS, daughter of Mary Octavia
Pierre Taylor. Writer, artist, educator, and cofounder of
Chicago's DuSable Museum of African-American History.

The most important lesson I learned from Mother was my
value system. These lessons include my belief in God and
the Christian principles of faith, hope, and charity; respect
for the rights of all people; the ethics by which I live and
work; a quest for knowledge and education; love of freedom
and independence; a thirst for justice; and dedication and
love of family and a sense of service. This value system is a
rich legacy which will always be the guiding force in my life.

—CORETTA SCOTT KING, daughter of Mrs. Bernice
McMurray Scott. Activist. From *Ebony*, May 1992.

Always follow your heart, and never forget where you came from. Always extend your hand to help others.

—JANET JACKSON, daughter of Kathleen Jackson. Entertainer. From *Essence*, September 1993.

Judge people by what they do to you or what you, yourself, see them do to others.

—LEAH M. WILCOX, daughter of Mildred Oliver Wilcox. Vice president, Player & Talent Relations, National Basketball Association.

My mother is a very strong lady with strong moral values. Let me give you an instance. My brother, sister, and I were almost always together because my mom worked. We had to stay together to look after each other. Once we had gone shopping and somebody gave us a penny too much and we brought it home. My mother made the three of us walk back and return it. Remember, town is five miles away. She said that at least one out of the three should have known better, and since we didn't, all three were punished. Let me tell you, you don't forget lessons like that.

—BRIGADIER GENERAL SHERIAN GRACE CADORIA,
daughter of Bernice McGlory Cadoria. One of the
highest-ranking African-American women in the
United States armed forces. From *I Dream a World*.

"Never mistreat anybody," she would say, "no matter how nasty they might be to you. They might be the very ones who are feeding you. We have to live from the people, and you have to show them your gratitude."

—CHARLAYNE HUNTER-GAULT, granddaughter of Alberta Hunter. Journalist. From *In My Place.*

My mother taught me how the light always illuminates the darkness, that the good always "win" in the end. She maintained the importance of being a good person, full of love, always thankful and generous.

She also showered us with African fables full of wisdom and speaking animals, reminding us to be strong and to act honestly without fear and anger.

—AYA, daughter of Marta Llerena. Fashion model.

I grew up in a family and an environment where opening doors for others and literally opening your front door to others was not only expected but practiced. Even though my sister and I grew up with a lot of advantages, my stepmother always stressed the importance of helping others and keeping your priorities straight. This wonderful woman married my father when I was four years old and is in every way the mother of my heart. Even today, she sends me short notes occasionally, reminding me to do what is right, remember what's important in life, and get some rest.

—HAZEL R. O'LEARY, daughter of Mattie R. Reid.

Give from your heart, and it will be returned ten times over.

> —BRENDA J. LAUDERBACK, daughter of Dorothy Lauderback.
> Group president, Nine West Group, Inc.

Life is short, and it's up to you to make it sweet.

> —SADIE DELANY, daughter of Nanny Logan Delany. Educator.
> From *Having Our Say.*

My mother always stressed the importance of speaking the truth. She often reminded my sister and me how important it was for her to know we would tell her the truth. She told me: "If others speak falsely about you, I can always respond that Eleanor has told me differently and I believe her."

There were several occasions when the importance of my words being my bond proved to be crucial when falsely accused. Consequently, I am committed to speaking the truth as honestly as I know that truth to be at any given time. My mother instilled in me the importance of speaking honestly but with kindness and gentleness. To this day, my sense of integrity is very important to me. It is the basis for an important part of my being and intricately tied to my leadership style.

—ELEANOR J. SMITH, daughter of Eleanor J. Lewis.
Chancellor, University of Wisconsin, Parkside.

Respectability, achievement, hard work—those were the values my parents lived by, and my mother worked hard to instill them in me.

> —DIAHANN CARROLL, daughter of Mabel Johnson.
> Entertainer. From her autobiography, *Diahann!*

My grandmother always told me—and when I was a young child showed me—that everyone was worth listening to, even the smallest child.

> —DR. ALEXA CANADY-DAVIS, granddaughter
> of Essie Mae Golden Pery. Became at age thirty
> the first African-American woman
> neurosurgeon in the country.

Give your best in service to the present and future society.
Help others to succeed.

—MARVALENE HUGHES, daughter of Alverta Hall Hughes,
President, California State University, Stanislaus.

*If we lose love and self-respect and respect
for each other, this is how we will finally die.*

—MAYA ANGELOU, daughter of Vivian Baxter.
Educator and author. From *Essence*, 1992.

Sturdy Black Bridges:
The Gift of Support

No matter how dark the circumstance, we could always depend on our mothers' support, to catch us in their safety net when we fell, to hold the ladder when we tried to reach new heights. Our mothers showed their support in so many ways, from the material possessions that they lovingly bestowed upon us in order to make our lives a little more comfortable, enjoyable, stylish, or secure to the more intangible support in the form of an emotional, unshakable, unbreakable bond.

Similar to wedding vows between a husband and wife, vows exist between a mother and daughter that, although never formalized in a ceremony, often endure the test of time. We can always rely upon the support of our mothers in good times and in bad, in sickness and in health, for richer or for poorer, for better or for worse, till death do us part.

And even upon death we know that Mom is waiting at heaven's gate with a warm meal, a mother's smile, and some juicy gossip.

My mother, religious-negro proud of,
having waded through a storm, is,
very obviously,
a sturdy Black bridge that I
crossed over, on.

—CAROLYN RODGERS, daughter of Bazella Colding. Author.
From *Songs of a Black Bird.*

I was a mute for five years. I wasn't cute and I didn't speak. I don't know what would have happened to me had I been in an integrated school. In another society, I'm sure I would have been ruled out. But my grandma told me all the time, "Sister, Mama don't care what these people say about you being a moron, being a idiot. Mama don't care. Mama know, Sister, when you and the good Lord get ready, you're gonna be a preacher."

—MAYA ANGELOU, granddaughter of Annie Henderson. Educator and author. From *I Dream a World.*

She was always encouraging me to sing. She told me to use my God-given talent. She said, "If you don't use it, God will give it to somebody else." She gave me birth, love, confidence, and constant direction.

—WHITNEY HOUSTON, daughter of Cissy Houston. Entertainer. From *Essence,* Spring 1990.

My mother is a quiet, private person and isn't one who lectures. I've learned from her by example. She has offered advice from the viewpoint of someone with experience (mother knows best . . .). Invariably she is right.

I learned from my mother how to be fair and kind, but also how to take care of myself. She is remarkably self-sufficient.

I think the greatest gift she had given me—by not warning me to be wary, suspicious, or biased—is the awareness that I'm capable of anything. I have, therefore, pursued all of my dreams with the confidence and assurance of a "warrioress" laying claim to the world. And I have succeeded. She now says she is proud of her beautiful children.

> —SANDRA ELAINE KITT, daughter of Annebelle Kitt. Considered
> the foremost African-American writer of romance novels.
> She has written more than a dozen books, most
> recently *The Color of Love.*

My mother's formal education was quite limited, but she was a very wise and compassionate person. She never discouraged my wildest dream and ambition to become an actress; but she did encourage me to provide myself with a "safety net," like a college education. If my dream of becoming an actress didn't come through, I would have other skills to fall back on. Momma believed in having a "Plan B"—just in case. . . . Oh, how I loved that lady. I can hear her telling me very sweetly whenever I got upset or opinionated, "Baby, don't take yourself so seriously."

—ROXIE ROKER, daughter of Bessie Roker.
Actor and mother of Lenny Kravitz.

I had a series of childhood illnesses. It started off as scarlet fever, and from there it was polio. My father was the one who sort of babied me and was sympathetic. He was a determined person. He had to be. There were twenty-two children. I am the twentieth. My mother was the one who made me work, made me believe that one day it would be possible for me to walk without braces.

—WILMA RUDOLPH, daughter of Blanche Rudolph. Three-time Olympic gold medalist. From *I Dream a World*.

One day in San Francisco, when I was 20 years old, I went to visit my mother, a visit that took place about once a month. She had cooked two of my favorite dishes and had offered me money. I always ate the food and I always refused the money.

At the end of the visit she accompanied me out of the house and down to the bottom of the hill. She offered me a ride in her big, beautiful, beige-and-tan Pontiac. Characteristically, I thanked her and refused. And then she spoke to me, and in her speech, liberated me forever: "I think you are the greatest woman I have ever met. You are kind and you are intelligent, and those two virtues rarely go together." She asked me for a kiss and walked south to her car, and I crossed the street east to the streetcar line.

I remember that day as vividly as if it happened yester-day. I remember how the sun fell into the windows and onto the slats of the streetcar benches. I remember thinking: "She is intelligent and she is too mean to lie. Suppose she is right; just suppose I'm really somebody."

I began to set my sights higher, my aspirations higher, my hopes higher. For on that day I believed that I might just reach the top.

> —MAYA ANGELOU, daughter of Vivian Baxter.
> Educator and author. From "How My Mother
> Changed My Life," *Ebony*, May 1993.

My mom told me to never let anyone tell me no. If I want something out of life . . . Go for it!!! When I first tried to model, four agencies told me, "No, thank you. We don't need another black girl, etc., etc. . . ." Well, I didn't listen to them. Thanks, Ma!

—TYRA BANKS, daughter of Carolyn London-Johnson. Fashion model and actor.

When I did the Free South Africa protest, my mother woke up Thanksgiving morning and saw on television that I was in jail. I called her and said, "Mom, I'm in jail." And she said, "Well, it's a good cause."

—MARY FRANCES BERRY, daughter of Frances Southall Berry. Historian, educator, attorney, activist, government official. From *I Dream a World*.

My mother never tried to force us to do anything. We have made our own choices, and I can really credit my mother for that because she never wanted to make a choice for us. She always let us make our own decisions, and so anything I do in connection with the King Center and my father's legacy, continuing his work, is something to which I feel a strong personal commitment.

—BERNICE ALBERTINE KING, daughter of Coretta Scott King. Baptist minister, lawyer, civil rights activist. From *Essence*, January 1989.

My mom, who passed away in 1988, was a woman of few words. She communicated her feelings in very subtle ways. Oftentimes it wasn't what she said as much as what she did. I do recall she told me to use my imagination. As a kid I really didn't understand what she meant. When I tried to learn to ride a two-wheeler, she said, "Imagine it." When I was in fifth grade and had to write, direct, and star in my own short play, she said, "Imagine it." It wasn't until after college that I understood the significance of her words. It wasn't to pre-tend, to hope, or to wish. She meant: If you focus, if you really believe and can envision your goal, you can obtain it or do it. I try to *visualize* whatever I want, not only the goal, but also all the steps to achieving that goal.

—WENDY FRYE, daughter of Emma H. Watts.
Product manager at Oscar Mayer.

"Just ignore people who try to pull you back. It's *their* problem. Remember, your father and I always love you and you can come back home if you ever need to. We will always be proud of you!" These are the words I remember when things get difficult. She is standing in the wings, cheering me on. I always feel her there.

—LINDA BEATRICE BROWN, daughter of Edith Brown.
Professor, and author of the novels *Rainbow
'Roun Mah Shoulder* and *Crossing Over Jordan*.

My mother always told me to listen to that little voice inside that's always struggling to maintain my peace of mind and to keep me moving *forward*. And if I wasn't moving forward, my mother inspired me by kicking me in my ass (figuratively) when needed.

—NADIRAH ZAKIYYAH SABÍR, daughter of
Ziyadah Shukriyyah Sabír. Editorial
researcher, *Black Enterprise.*

I am very fortunate to be the daughter of an incredible mother. As a single parent, she emotionally, physically, and financially supported my brother and myself. She has been my greatest inspiration in life. She always made me believe that I could be anything I wanted to be as long as I kept God in my life. She supported me in decisions that "society" would probably deem wrong—I dropped out of college, married at eighteen, and had my daughter at twenty. I feel her smile from heaven surround me constantly.

—VIVIAN L. SCOTT, daughter of Mamie L. Murphy.
Executive vice president, Sony Music.

I cannot forget my mother. Though not as sturdy as others, she is my bridge. When I needed to get across, she steadied herself long enough for me to run across safely. For that I am grateful.

> —RENITA WEEMS, daughter of Carrie Baker Weems.
> Author. From "Hush, Mama's Gotta Go Bye-Bye,"
> *Double Stitch.*

My mother died when I was one year old, but my grandmother raised me from one to six years of age. I was a tomboy when I was very little and everyone complained about me running outside with the boys, tearing up my pretty little dresses. But mama, my grandmother, used to say: "Just let my baby be. She ain't like the others. She rough. She'll stumble on gentleness later on."

> —SONIA SANCHEZ, granddaughter of Elizabeth Driver and
> daughter of Lena Jones Driver. Professor, and author of
> fourteen books including *Home Girls and Handgrenades*,
> *Under a Soprano Sky*, and *Wounded in the House of a Friend.*

My mother's most memorable words of advice were said to me just before I left home at eighteen to go to Paris to start my modeling career: "Follow your dreams, sweetheart. If you fall, I'll be there to catch you."

—ROSHUMBA WILLIAMS, daughter of LaVonne Joslin. Fashion model.

My mother was always someone who never laughed at my mistakes, who shared my pain and joys, who always stood beside me, never in front or behind me. She was as strong as an oak and yet as gentle as the morning dew, as beautiful as the sunset—and still is.

> —ORNETTA BARBER DICKERSON, daughter of Edna Morales.
> Vice president, Black Music Marketing,
> Warner/Elektra/Atlantic records.

My mom always taught us that family's all you have when everything's said and done. You have to love them and support them no matter who they are, no matter how they look, no matter how they may behave.

> —TONI BRAXTON, daughter of Evelyn Braxton.
> Singer. From *Jet*, May 1994.

"Me and daddy love you, baby, no matter
what happens. Always remember that."
My mother passed away on December 8,
1994, and these cherished words of her love
will always remain with me just as they did
when she was physically present in my life.
Momi declared her love for me during the
good and difficult times of my life, and these
words have been and will always remain my
sense of blessed strength.

—JULIA A. BOYD, daughter of Lavada (Jimmalee) Conyers.
Psychotherapist and author of *In the Company of My Sisters* and
Girlfriend to Girlfriend.

By no amount of agile exercising of a wishful imagination could my mother have been called lenient. Generous she was; indulgent, never. Kind, yes; permissive, never. In her world, people she accepted paddled their own canoes, pulled their own weight, put their own shoulders to their own plows and pushed like hell.

—MAYA ANGELOU, daughter of Vivian Baxter. Educator and author. From *Gather Together in My Name*.

She would always say to us, "Anything that happens, you can confide in Mama. Mama loves each child the way God loves His children. Nothing's too bad to tell Mama. Don't ever tell me a lie. It's not necessary, because Mama will understand."

> —SADIE DELANY, daughter of Nanny Logan Delany.
> Educator. From *Having Our Say*.

This has been the year that I have pushed hard against some of the rules of the "good daughter" and learned to really hear the message my mother has given me all my life: "I will be with you always." As in forever, into the eternal here-after, no matter what.

> —REBECCA WALKER, daughter of Alice Walker.
> Author. From *Essence*, May 1995.

R-E-S-P-E-C-T:
The Gift of Pride

If there was one recurring theme that our mothers consistently echoed, it was to be proud. Be proud of your race, be proud of your family, and most importantly be proud of yourself. This sense of pride was particularly pertinent when it came to confronting racism.

I was taught that racism was by consent, even if it was on a subliminal basis. I had to give the bigot permission to invade my mind. My mother reasoned that the more I knew about my race, the prouder I would be and the less likely I would knowingly let racism poison my mind and erode my self-esteem.

I am proud not only of my race. I am equally proud of my family, because it is hardworking, God-fearing families like mine that compose the majority of the human race. No one had ever handed anything on a silver platter to my mother or grandmother. In contrast, they sold home-grown crops in the local marketplace or cleaned bedpans to secure the few possessions they had. They were very proud of these possessions.

However, they kept their pride in check. You see, they were never too proud to accept other people's generosity if it meant a better life for their children. Although I was embarrassed to wear hand-me-down clothes from my neighbor, my mother always reminded me that "one man's rags are another man's riches." Furthermore, I should be thankful that once again "the Lord had provided." And the clothes that I could no longer wear were "provided" to others.

Ironically, this lesson in swallowing one's pride became increasingly valuable over the years as I shopped in thrift stores to make ends meet during college. Little did I know that I was in the vanguard of a fashion trend!

Gal, be proud of your color.

—CYNTHIA McKINNEY, great-granddaughter of Annie Bell Dixon.
Member of the U.S. Congress, representing Georgia's
11th congressional district (Democrat).

"I come from five generations of people who were slaves and sharecroppers—but ain't nobody in my family never let anybody pay 'em no money that was a way of telling us we wasn't fit to walk the earth. We ain't never been that poor."

> —Mama, from the play *A Raisin in the Sun*
> by LORRAINE HANSBERRY, daughter of
> Nannie Perry Hansberry.

My mother, Leona McCauley, helped me to grow up feeling proud of myself and other black people, even while living under racist conditions. She taught me not to judge people by the amount of money they had or the kind of house they lived in or the clothes they wore. People should be judged, she told me, by the respect they have for themselves and others. Her advice helped me to do the hard things that I had to do later in life.

> —ROSA PARKS, daughter of Leona McCauley.
> Activist. From *Quiet Strength*.

My mother was a great woman. She went through a lot of suffering to bring the twenty of us up, but she still taught us to be decent and to respect ourselves, and that is one of the things that has kept me going.

—FANNIE LOU HAMER, daughter of Lou Ella Townsend. Activist. From the biography *This Little Light of Mine*.

My parents taught me to be the best human being I could be. They told me that it was wonderful that I was Black and that if I did my best I would be rewarded.

—LEONTYNE PRICE, daughter of Kate Baker Price. Opera diva. From *Essence*, Spring 1990.

"Depend on yourself. Always depend on yourself." How often did my sister and I hear those words when we were growing up. If our husbands abandoned us or died, we had to be able to take care of ourselves. Hence [my mother's] emphasis on education.

"Feed your mind. Feed your mind." Those words, too, we heard on a daily basis. Ideas, she taught us, were more important than things.

"Never envy anybody," because it takes you away from caring for yourself.

We had to live our lives in such a way that if anybody defamed our character, they would be lying, and the whole world would know they were lying. "All you'll ever have in this life is your own integrity. Don't ever give it up for anything or anybody."

> —GLORIA WADE-GAYLES, daughter of Bertha Wade.
> Author. From her autobiography,
> *Pushed Back to Strength*.

Deal with yourself as an individual worthy of respect, and make everyone else deal with you the same way.

> —NIKKI GIOVANNI, daughter of Yolanda Giovanni.
> Poet and activist. From *Proud Sisters*.

I remember telling my mother one day. I said, "Mother, how come we are not white? Because white people have clothes, they can have food to eat, and we work all the time and we don't have anything."

She said, "I don't ever want you to say that again, honey." She said, "Don't you say that, because you're black!" She said, "You respect yourself as a little child, a little black child. And as you grow older, respect yourself as a black woman. Then one day, other people will respect you."

—FANNIE LOU HAMER, daughter of Lou Ella Townsend. Activist. From *This Little Light of Mine.*

If you hold your head up and never look down, people will think you're somebody.

—GLORIA WADE-GAYLES, granddaughter of Proud Nola. Author. From her autobiography, *Pushed Back to Strength.*

Get up in the front of the line—don't let them get in front of you.

—KIMBERLEY HATCHETT, daughter of Ora Hatchett. Investment manager, Morgan Stanley.

Racial tensions created an atmosphere of fear, yet there was courage; they created a sense of powerlessness, yet there was determination. My grandmother survived and reared her daughter to survive. My mother reared me to survive in her own fashion. She gave me heroes and heroines to be proud of. She told me about George W. Carver, Joe Louis, Booker T. Washington, Paul Lawrence Dunbar (for whom my father was named), Phyllis Wheatley, Madame Walker, and others. She taught me how to turn away wrath with a soft answer but without letting anybody make me think I was inferior to them.

> —ANNETTE JONES WHITE, daughter of Delores Berry Jones.
> Author. From "Dyad/Triad," *Double Stitch*.

She truly believed that "everybody was somebody and ain't nobody shit."

> —GLORIA WADE-GAYLES, daughter of Bertha Wade.
> Author. From "Connected to Mama's Spirit,"
> *Double Stitch*.

The way I was taught, being black was a plus, always. Being a human being, being in America, and being black, all three were the greatest things that could happen to you. The combination was unbeatable.

—LEONTYNE PRICE, daughter of Kate Baker Price.
Opera diva. From *I Dream A World.*

"Everybody, his brother and his dog, thinks he can walk a road in a colored woman's behind. But you remember this, now. Your mother raised you. You're full-grown. Let them catch it like they find it. If you haven't been trained at home to their liking tell them to get to stepping. . . . Stepping. But not on you."

—MAYA ANGELOU, daughter of Vivian Baxter.
Educator and author. From *Gather Together in My Name.*

Go On, Girl!
The Gift of Inspiration

Our mothers have always served as an inspiration to us, perhaps because the catalyst for much of their behavior is based on love and the drive to succeed. We have been blessed to have each of them as our role models. For despite the almost insurmountable odds that they had to overcome, they did it with so much pride and dignity—never forgetting their roots.

Through her example, my mother always inspired me. She would often say with much pride and vigor, "What I have accomplished is worth a Ph.D." For although she did not formally receive a doctorate from an institution of higher learning, in her mind she had earned one through the school of hard knocks. While the village elders when she was a child in Jamaica had assumed she would rightfully accept her preordained destiny to marry young, raise a family, harvest the crops, and care for her aging mother, my mother had plans of her own to become a nurse in a foreign land far from Jamaica. Despite the social and financial odds against her, she single-handedly put herself through nursing school, working the night shift at a tin factory in London. And as a single mother, she tried to ensure that I had the best care available even though that meant leaving me with my Aunt Daphne for seven years. And as the years passed on, my mother constantly worked the overtime shift to make up any shortfall.

So whenever I'm feeling blue and sorry for myself, I think of my mother and all that she has accomplished despite the odds against her. In comparison, my life has been a bowl of cherries. Yes, Mom, you have graduated from the school of hard knocks with an honorary Ph.D. in Inspiration!

Set yourself a goal and reach it.
Take what you have and make what you want.

—MARION TAYLOR HUMMONS, daughter of Mary Octavia Pierre Taylor. Cofounder of Chicago's DuSable Museum of African-American History.

You can be anything that you want to be, but remember it's not going to be easy. You must work hard, and when things get tough—and they will—and it looks as if you're not going to make it, keep pushing just a little harder. Never give up. Even if you get knocked down you must get back up, because one thing's for sure, you can never beat someone who is willing to go one more round.

—KATHY RUSSELL, daughter of Dorothy Clarese Russell.
Author of *The Color Complex: The Politics of Skincolor Among African-Americans* and *Divided Sisters: Bridging the Gap between Black Women and White Women.*

She taught me the importance of self-reliance, self-respect, and self-discipline. She believed, as I do, that having these characteristic traits, there was nothing I couldn't accomplish in life.

She inspired me to be a great human being and to treat people as I would want them to treat me. She instilled in me to never take anything for granted, because life is a precious gift, and the gift of life shouldn't be misused, but treasured.

I hope through my existence, the world sees how my mother truly inspired me to be a great person.

—JACKIE JOYNER-KERSEE, daughter of Mary Joyner. Olympic gold medalist. From *Ebony*, May 1993.

I learned from my mother not to be afraid. She was a very courageous person, and I could see her in action doing many things there on Henrietta Street. She had a way of letting you know that she was never afraid of anyone, and she wanted you to be able to stand your ground regardless of where you were or whatever happened. . . . I really feel that it helped me to be able to stand in front of the Klansmen and the White Citizens' Councils, of large groups that were hostile. I never felt afraid, and I think it was due to the fact that my mother showed so much courage back in those days. I felt that if she could do it way back then, then I could.

> —SEPTIMA CLARK, daughter of Victoria Warren Anderson Poinsette. Activist. From *Ready from Within: Septima Clark and the Civil Rights Movement.*

My parents gave me stability and a belief in myself and in all the possibilities life has to offer. I was told the only limitations I would ever face were those I placed upon myself. Being a black woman was never considered an obstacle, which is why I believe that if there is something I want to do and I am willing to work for it, the door, *any* door, will open.

> —DIONNE WARWICK, daughter of Lee Warrick. Singer. From *Essence*, May 1991.

My mother has taught me that "anything that the mind can conceive and believe, it most definitely can achieve." Empowering words, which serve as the foundation for most of what I do.

> —DYANA WILLIAMS, daughter of Professor Nancy Vives Neuman. President, International Association of African-American Music.

My mother was the backbone of our family. Even my father went to her for advice and inspiration. When I was sixteen years old, my mother heard me sing live for the first time professionally. From the stage I could see her crying and truly moved. This inspired me to go on. She told me later that if this is really what I wanted to do not to worry about trying to change all the things around me. She said to just go on and pray, and I'd have the strength to change what was within me to get where I wanted to be. She said you can't change everything around you, but you can change yourself and get where you want to go. Just make up your mind.

> —DENISE TICHENOR, daughter of Dorothy L. Tichenor. Gospel singer. Hailed as the "Patti LaBelle of Gospel Music."

She taught me that she was my friend as well as my mother by exposing me to the variety in life—church, opera, the blues, and the mix of children's and adult literature. She recited to me Latin phrases, Longfellow, and Paul Lawrence Dunbar. She showed me photographs of Albert Einstein, Percy Julian, and Paul Robeson. She took me to hear the Boston Pops, the Mills Brothers, Ella Fitzgerald, and Cab Calloway. She bought me books on every occasion. She told me that I could be whatever I wanted to be. . . . And I believed her!

> —DR. SHIRLEY ANN REDD LEWIS, daughter of
> Mrs. Thelma Biggers Redd. First woman
> president of Paine College.

"Remember, nobody promised you anything," used to be the way my grandmother usually ended her conversations with me when I was growing up. An incredibly beautiful, large, enormously charismatic woman, she would say, "We can give you love, straight teeth, and a good brain. No one can take what's in your head away from you. The rest is up to you." In a way, because I expected nothing to be easy and nothing to be given, I believed everything was possible. This not only gave me confidence but security and perhaps even the serenity to expect a lot out of life.

Making one's own luck was very important to both my grandmother and my mother. My mother's favorite exhortation was that "doing things without giving the impression of suffering was a question of good manners." Letting the world know you were carrying a heavy burden was, she would say, "a third-world attitude toward life." Imagine my delight when, thirty years later, in Turin, Italy, I heard the president of Fiat, Gianni Agnelli, explain his success as the top European automaker in exactly the same words—in Italian! Race, gender, nationality were all different, but the idea was universal: pride, independence, world-class excellence, and remember your manners. . . .

—BARBARA CHASE-RIBOUD, daughter of Vivian Braithwaite
West Chase and granddaughter of Elizabeth Johnson
Chase. Author of four best-selling books including
Sally Hemings and its sequel, *The President's Daughter.*

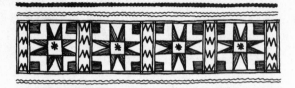

My mother always said you can do whatever you want to. She always went after whatever she wanted and instilled that in me. She's very strong, very opinionated, never holds back.

—VANESSA WILLIAMS, daughter of Helen Williams. Entertainer. From *Essence*, August 1994.

My mom never told me I couldn't do anything, and I guess that's why I've done a lot of things.

—DEBBYE TURNER, daughter of Gussie Turner. Miss America 1990. From *Essence*, January 1990.

To believe in myself, to believe that I could do anything that I wanted to do—anything as long as I put my mind to it, and to always say my prayers.

—DANA OWENS, (aka Queen Latifah), daughter of Rita Owens. Entertainer. From *Jet*, May 9, 1994.

Never accept less in life than living it to the fullest.

—BRENDA J. LAUDERBACK, daughter of Dorothy Lauderback. Group president, Nine West Group, Inc.

The School of Hard Knocks: The Gift of Perseverance

No matter what, our mothers taught us to never give up and to face adversity head on with a clear mind and a strong vision. In my family, like most other families, generations of Cooper women experienced adversity in one form or another. For example, despite losing her husband at a young age, my grandmother single-handedly raised nine rambunctious children in the Jamaican mountains. Each child pursued a career and established him- or herself successfully.

And, although pregnant out-of-wedlock in an era when such a "condition" brought shame on a family, my mother proudly gave birth to me and then had to leave me with relatives so she could establish a life for us. The emotional tug-of-war from the seven-year separation haunted her soul. Her only comfort comes with the thoughts that she did the best for me that she knew how; by realizing her dream she would clear the path for me to realize my dreams.

And, although I was diagnosed with a reading problem at the age of nine, my mother refused to let this so-called disability stymie my future. Instead, I was inundated with books, dictionaries, and magazines as well as enrolled in special reading classes. I diligently attended these classes twice a week from fourth through sixth grades—never once missing a session. By the time I was in seventh grade I was devouring books, everything from Richard Wright to Jacqueline Suzanne. Thus, it came as no surprise to my mother when my seventh-grade English teacher reported that I was reading on an eleventh-grade level.

My grandmother and my mom and I overcame adversity through determination and perseverance, as did all of the mothers and daughters in this book. Their stories of facing down the "hard knocks" that came their way are stories and examples that inspire us when we face similar "hard knocks."

"Never say *can't.*" When it was said, it was proved that whatever you "couldn't" do, you did!

—LESLIE M. SEGAR (aka Big Lez), daughter of Ella P. Segar. Music video dancer, choreographer, and on-air host of BET's "Rap City."

Give in, but don't give up.

—CARRIE P. MEEK, daughter of Carrie Tansy Pittman. Former teacher, granddaughter of a slave, and a member of the U.S. Congress, representing Florida's 17th congressional district in Miami (Democrat).

When things go wrong, you must pray, keep the faith, and don't stop working hard.

—ANITA DOREEN DIGGS, daughter of Gladys Haigler-Smith. Author of *Talking Drums* and *Success at Work.*

I can remember when I was a little girl, how my old mammy would sit out of doors in the evenings and look up at the stars and groan, and I would say, "Mammy, what makes you groan so?" And she would say, "I am groaning to think of my poor children; they do not know where I be and I don't know where they be. I look up at the stars and they look up at the stars!"

—SOJOURNER TRUTH, daughter of Elizabeth Mau-Mau Bett Baumfree. Activist. From *Narrative of Sojourner Truth.*

In everyone's life, a little rain must fall; *but* every cloud has a silver lining!

—CI CI HOLLOWAY, daughter of Joan Holloway. Senior vice president, Viacom Interactive Media, and founder of Vista Records.

My grandma always impressed upon me to never accept defeat or bow to obstacles in my path. My mantra is her voice saying, "There's more than one way to skin a cat."

> —TONYA PINKINS, granddaughter of Ollie Mae
> Christopher. Tony-nominated actor in the Broadway
> play *Smokey Joe's Cafe*.

When the going gets rough, the tough get tougher and the weak fall by the wayside. . . . A winner never quits and a quitter never wins.

> —DR. ANDREE NICOLA MCLAUGHLIN, daughter of
> Willie Mae Newman McLaughlin. Professor,
> Medgar Evers College, and author of *Wild
> Women in the Whirlwind: Afra-American
> Culture and the Contemporary
> Literary Renaissance*.

Having been a pregnant teenager forced into marriage by her parents, Mother felt, and still feels, the most important lesson in life is to make the best of that which comes your way. Whether good or bad, seek the lessons that can come out of the experience and then strive for advancement from that point forward, using every mental, spiritual, and physical resource available.

She also proffers the theory that when alone or lonely without benefit of a mentor, seek the courage to stand on your own and trust your judgment of right and wrong to lead you forward.

This seems to have worked for her, this housewife and mother of eight grateful and appreciative children.

—ANDREA ARCENEAUX, daughter of O. Olivia Arceneaux. Anchorperson, "Early Edition," CNN.

Run, run, run until you can't run anymore.

> —KIMBERLEY HATCHETT, daughter of Ora Hatchett.
> Investment manager, Morgan Stanley.

I had very strong women role models in my mother, my grandmother, and my aunt. They used to say, "When you fall down, get up. If you fall down again, get up. And don't be ashamed of falling down."

> —CARRIE SAXON PERRY, daughter of Mabel Lee Saxon.
> First African-American woman elected mayor of a
> major U.S. city (Hartford, CT). From *I Dream a World*.

I've always looked at the more positive side of things. All the pain I've had in my life, I'll hold on to it for a second and then I'll let it go. I really try to let go of all the negativity and leave the rest up to God. That's one of the beautiful gifts my mother gave me, the ability to allow certain things to be.

> —DIANA ROSS, daughter of Ernestine Ross. Entertainer.
> From her autobiography, *Secrets of a Sparrow*.

You can cry and feel sorry for yourself . . . or you can dry your eyes and get on with your life. If you take mess, you're asking for it, and you'll get it. Don't be no fool, woman. You can change your life. It's about will. If you will something to happen and work at it, it can happen.

> —GLORIA WADE-GAYLES, daughter of Bertha Wade. Author.
> From "Connected to Mama's Spirit," *Double Stitch*.

Failure?
I'm not ashamed to tell it,
I never learned to spell it,
Not Failure.

> —MAYA ANGELOU, daughter of Vivian Baxter.
> Educator and author. From her poem
> "Call Letters: Mrs. V.B."

The reward is not so great without the struggle. . . . The triumph can't be had without the struggle.

> —WILMA RUDOLPH, daughter of Blanche Rudolph. Three-time
> Olympic gold medalist. From the *Chicago Tribune*.

If the first woman God ever made was strong enough to turn the world upside down all alone, these women together ought to be able to turn it back, and get it right side up again.

> —SOJOURNER TRUTH, daughter of Elizabeth Mau-Mau
> Bett Baumfree. Activist. From her address to the Ohio
> Women's Rights Convention, 1851.

You may encounter many defeats, but you must not be defeated.

> —MAYA ANGELOU, daughter of Vivian Baxter. Educator and author.
> From *The Black 100*.

It Takes a Village to
Raise a Child:
The Gift of Community

Just as our ancestors left young ones with community elders so they could hunt, fish, and till the soil, our mothers left us under the watchful eyes of relatives and neighbors so they could put a roof over our heads, food on the table, and clothes on our backs.

These extended family members always leaned out the windows or sat on the stoops, watching out for us while mama was away. How often we heard their warning, "Look both ways before crossing the street," or their guilt-ridden question, "Child, what would your mama say if she saw you doing that?" Good or bad, watching or snitching, these extended family members helped nurture us by being role models or surrogate mothers. How rich our community of family is. How blessed we are.

How blessed we are that our race's elders—women such as Ida B. Wells-Barnett, Sojourner Truth, Mary McLeod Bethune, Mary Church Terrell, Frances Harper, Anna Julia

Cooper—shared their words of wisdom, their life's experiences. How blessed we are to have their life's deeds and triumphs to lift us as we climbed, to raise us to believe all the world can be ours if we just believe in our strength. How blessed we are to have the women who appear on the following pages, sitting on the stoops in our minds, raising and inspiring generations upon generations of women with their words, actions, deeds, and examples.

My sisters, the time has come to take an even closer look at the role of education in the empowerment of African-American women, realizing that when we are empowered, so, too, will be all African-Americans. Although the logic behind this is obvious, it bears repeating: Women are the primary caretakers of children and, consequently, their first teachers. So, as they say, when you educate a man you educate an individual, but when you educate a woman, you educate a nation. This is why we must learn and we must teach. If we need role models, we can certainly look to our foremothers.

Remember that nameless West African woman who represented all our foremothers. Despite grueling work and ignominious abuse, she became both a student and a teacher. She recognized her powerment. First she taught herself a new language. It certainly was not the standard American English of the time, but it was at least enough to communicate with her slavekeepers and fellow slaves. And in this her motives were quite simple: Language would at least give her the power to name things in her captor's own words. This woman studied "white folks' ways," not in any grotesque desire to emulate them, but in order to recognize and anticipate the many faces of oppression, brutality, and cruelty.

One of the most invaluable contributions this woman made to her community was in her efforts to train her children. By passing her knowledge on, she expressed a willingness to embrace the future and a strong unwillingness to accept her horrible condition as hopeless and unchangeable. This woman was a teacher. It is wonderfully romantic to think she consciously and actively taught her children African history and culture, but such was neither practical nor reasonable. Her lessons were much more basic, much more survival-oriented. This woman taught important life-and-death lessons. She taught her children to be alert when whites were present and to study their faces just as she did. She taught them to plant codes in the songs they sang and secret gardens in the woods. She gave swift, practical lessons, designed to impart information. She stole snatches of formal education from the slaveholder's children. But formal education was not at the core of the African woman's teachings. She taught what we still refer to as Mother Wit. In slavequarter churches and secret, forbidden meetings, she preached the principles of survival and such survival tools as herbal medicine and North Star navigation. She taught the art of endurance and the beginning of resistance.

This nameless West African woman who survived the Middle Passage, who lived in spite of slavery, somehow found the courage and the righteous indignation to struggle for a future she knew she would never see. She chose to endure and determined in her mind not to surrender, but for her own sake and the sake of generations to follow to keep her will and her soul alive. This nameless West African woman is a giant on whose shoulders all of us stand.

—JOHNNETTA B. COLE, daughter of Mary Frances Lewis Betsch.
First woman president, Spelman College. From *Conversations*.

I am ever mindful of the fact that the groups I belong to—African-American people, women people—are still in the process of pulling the gags out of our mouths; that in speaking freely and publicly, in expressing our thoughts and feelings, we do so as much for our ancestors and foremothers as we do for ourselves.

—MARCIA ANN GILLESPIE. Former editor in chief of *Essence* and current editor in chief of *Ms. Magazine.*
From *Proud Sisters.*

It is the responsibility of every adult—especially parents, educators, and religious leaders—to make sure that children hear what we have learned from the lessons of life, and to hear over and over that we love them and that they are not alone.

> —MARIAN WRIGHT EDELMAN, daughter of Maggie Leola Wright.
> President, Children's Defense League. From *African-American
> Woman Quote Book.*

And so lifting as we climb, onward and upward as we go, struggling and striving and hoping that the buds and blossoms of our desires will burst into glorious fruition ere long. With courage born of success achieved in the past, with a keen sense of responsibility, which we must continue to assume, we look forward to the future, large with promise and hope. Seeking no favors because of our color or patronage because of our needs, we knock at the bar of justice and ask for an equal chance.

> —MARY CHURCH TERRELL, daughter of Louisa Ayers.
> Suffragist. From "What Role Is the Educated Negro
> Woman to Play in the Uplifting of Her Race?"

I was about eight years old and I opened the door one day, and there was Mary McLeod Bethune. I remember sitting on the floor playing as my mother and she talked. Mrs. Bethune was saying that colored women need to stop playing bridge and start building bridges.

—LEONTINE T. C. KELLY, daughter of Ila Turpeau. First black woman bishop of a major religious denomination, the United Methodist Church, in the United States. From *I Dream a World.*

There is a place in God's sun for the youth "farthest down" who has the vision, the determination, and the courage to reach it.

—MARY McLEOD BETHUNE, daughter of Patsy McIntosh McLeod. Activist and educator . From *Words to Make My Dream Children Live.*

*African-American women can do anything
that they set out to do.*

—JOHNNETTA COLE, daughter of Mary Frances Betsch. First woman
president of Spelman College. From *Epic Lives.*

God wields national judgment on national sins.

—FRANCES ELLEN WATKINS HARPER. Activist.
From *Letter to John Brown,* 1859.

*Though it be a thrilling marvelous thing to be
merely young and gifted in such times, it is
doubly so, doubly dynamic—to be young,
gifted and black. Look at the work
that awaits you!*

—LORRAINE HANSBERRY, daughter of Nannie Perry Hansberry.
Playwright. From *To Be Young, Gifted and Black.*

You know I work for the liberation of all
people, because when I liberate myself,
I'm liberating other people.

—FANNIE LOU HAMER, daughter of Lou Ella Townsend. Activist.
From *Proud Sisters.*

"Be proud and draw on your strength. Lord knows you're stubborn enough, but don't be scared to give your strength and your love to your people. Give it away. Believe in yourself and your people, because finally, that's all you got."

—HERMINE PINSON, granddaughter of Grandma Yetta.
Professor, the College of William and Mary, and poet.

"Jump at de Sun":
The Gift of Dreams

Mothers always dream that life will be better for their daughters than it was for them; they believe that with a little luck and a lot of guidance, their daughters can live more fulfilling and rewarding lives.

Our mothers, in turn, encourage us to share in their dreams as well as create our own dreams. They know that dreams ignite a drive to succeed. No matter how absurd our dreams are, our mothers somehow make them seem achievable—"If you can dream it, you can be it!" I heard my mother declare. Oftentimes, she embellished my dreams, making them grander. "Why be a nurse when you can be a doctor? Why be the student when you can be the teacher? Why be the First Lady when you can be the President?" she challenged me and challenged me and challenged me.

In order to further these dreams, our mothers often enrolled us in tap class or summer school. Whatever it took! Anything to fuel the imagination, to spur us on to make our dreams realities. As Alice Walker writes, "And for the three magic gifts I needed to escape the poverty of my hometown, I thank my mother, who gave me a sewing machine, a typewriter, and a suitcase."

Although many of the dreams our mothers had for themselves never came to be, one hopes they can share in our dreams as they become realities. For it is mothers who really do make dreams come true.

Mama exhorted her children at every opportunity to "jump at de sun." We might not land on the sun, but at least we would get off the ground.

—ZORA NEALE HURSTON, daughter of Lucy Ann Potts Hurston. Author. From her autobiography, *Dust Tracks on a Road*.

In my world, black women can do anything.

—JULIE DASH, daughter of Rhudine Dash. Filmmaker and director
of *Daughters of the Dust.* From *Proud Sisters.*

"You ain't going to work in Mister Charley's kitchen like me. I don't want you to go into service. You not going to be a scullery maid. We're going to fix it so you be something else than that."

—DOROTHY DANDRIDGE, daughter of Ruby Dandridge.
Entertainer. From her autobiography,
Everything and Nothing.

Reach for the stars—even if you fall short,
you will have stretched your potential.

—BRENDA J. LAUDERBACK, daughter of Dorothy Lauderback.
Group president, Nine West Group, Inc.

Pursue your dreams. Work as hard at it as you can, but always have a backup plan.

—ANITA DOREEN DIGGS, daughter of Gladys Haigler-Smith.
Author of *Talking Drums* and *Success at Work*.

My mother, Marion Lewis Redd, was a classically trained pianist and a music educator in Washington, D.C. She would have been a concert pianist if such a career had been available to a black woman in her time. But that was her dream. My mother had the gift of dreaming. She dreamed she saw the name Veronica Redd up in lights on a marquee, and that's how I got my name. I was painfully shy as a child, but my mother would have none of that. Though the Washington of her childhood and of mine was racially segregated, my mother went everywhere in search of cultural enrichment and took me with her. She taught me to be at ease in any social or public setting because it felt natural to be there. . . . I belonged there. She gave me piano, voice, dance, and drama lessons and thrust me into the limelight at every opportunity until that, too, became second nature to me. She died when I was eighteen, but my mother left me with the gift of dreams: the gift to dare to dream and the foundation upon which to build dreams. My mother poured her dreams into me and, after her death, it became my mission in life to live them.

—VERONICA REDD FORREST, daughter of Marion Lewis Redd. Veteran performer and TV producer, and one of the stars of *The Young and the Restless*. From *The Gift of Dreams*, a one-woman show, by Veronica Redd Forrest and Tone Forrest.

My mother always told me how important dreams are. "Never give up on your dreams, because dreams are where reality begins," she said.

—MARCIA Y. MAHAN, daughter of Mary Mahan. Editor, *Jive* and *Intimacy* magazines.

My mother wanted me to be a star and I worked hard for her goal.

—LENA HORNE, daughter of Edna Scottron Horne. Singer. From her autobiography, *Lena*.

Follow your dreams wherever they may lead. And always be yourself and do what makes you happy.

—RENEE WILLIAMS, daughter of Alberta Williams. Marketing manager, Citibank.

My mother felt that I should be a missionary nurse. Her dream for me was to go abroad to Africa and other parts of the world to serve the suffering. I have been something of a disappointment to her ideal, but, I think, from my own view, I have done missionary work nonetheless.

> —FAYE WATTLETON, daughter of Ozie Wattleton.
> First woman to head the nation's largest family-planning agency, Planned Parenthood.
> From *I Dream a World*.

When I envision the future, I think of the world I crave for my daughters and my sons. It is thinking for survival of the species—thinking for life.

> —AUDRE LORDE, daughter of Linda Belmar Lorde.
> Poet, activist, author. From *African-American Woman Quote Book*.

And for the three magic gifts I needed to escape the poverty of my hometown, I thank my mother, who gave me a sewing machine, a typewriter, and a suitcase. . . .

> —ALICE WALKER, daughter of Minnie Tallulah Grant Walker.
> Author. From *In Search of Our Mothers' Gardens.*

"Keep your eyes on the prize. Move on." That was Mama's philosophy. Set a goal for yourself, keep your eye on it, and "you'll get there." In the prime of health, I was now stronger than Mama but not as wise or brave. She had a way of seeing around sharp corners, over high fences, beneath thick layers of confusion and uncertainty to the very center of truth and practicality. She has a "single eye," she would tell my sister and me. "A single eye." That "eye" was focused on my sister and me, on our wholeness, our ability to stand tall in the light of our own suns.

> —GLORIA WADE-GAYLES, daughter of Bertha Wade.
> Author. From "Connected to Mama's Spirit,"
> *Double Stitch.*

My mother had a dream . . .

Amazon-style, she gripped a broom handle across her chest,
Its spear threatening to kiss my eyebrow.

This was not part of my mother's dream.

Mommy was proud of never hitting us, but
Deference
Would not, and could not be a part of this dream born
July 29, 1972.

She whispered, through tears, elbow braced against the
doorway.
"You, at 2 a.m., may not leave my home."

It did not matter that I was legally an adult, or that I'd lived
at college for a year.
All that mattered is that she never let her dreams go unchal-
lenged.

Her love was willing to prevent my pain at any cost.
I am still learning, and graciously, Mommy is still teaching.

Thank you, Mom.

I didn't give you cause to salute me with an upside-down
broom that day,
or any other.

But you really wouldn't have hit me.
Would you?

Maybe she won't go down in history for going back to college together with me. Or for raising three dreams—as she said, with Mommy-magic—who are also her friends. I am proud to be my mother's dream, and spend every day working to be one-third the woman she is.

> —ABIOLA WENDEE ABRAMS, daughter of Norma Abrams.
> Poet and performer.

We wanted something for ourselves and for our children, so we took a chance with our lives.

> —UNITA BLACKWELL. Activist. From *Famous Black Quotations*.

*There is enough power for everyone. Share it
and promulgate the dream.*

—MARVALENE HUGHES, daughter of Alverta Hall Hughes.
President, California State University, Stanislaus.

AMEN!: The Gift of Faith

Faith has played such a pivotal role in many of our lives. Our earliest childhood memories have God entwined in them. . . . Saturday night baths were in preparation for church the next day; meals could not start unless grace was said; sleep could not be had without a prayer first.

God was omnipresent. No matter what we did or where we went, God was always by our side. We dared not pick peaches off the neighbor's tree, curse our mother in private, or kiss a boy in the alley, because God was watching us.

No matter how hard my mother worked, it seemed as though a day would not go by without her reading the Bible, even if it was only for five minutes. Oftentimes, she would fall asleep from pure exhaustion with the Bible still in her hands. That Great Book guided her through many turbulent waters and served to comfort her in times of despair. She could always find the answers to her most difficult questions in the Bible. When you got right down to it, the answer seemed to always be "the Lord will provide."

Although we did not realize it as children, our mother's religion grounded us in ethics, morals, and values. It's not surprising that altruism is prevalent throughout the African-American community. No matter how down and out we are, we share our meager morsels with those in need, because we know "the Lord will provide," and each of us will be held accountable come Judgment Day.

My mother told me that I had "nobody in the wide world to look to but God."

—ELIZABETH. From her *Memoir of Old Elizabeth, a Coloured Woman*, 1863.

One needs occasionally to stand aside from the hum and rush of human interests and passions to hear the voices of God.

> —ANNA JULIA COOPER, daughter of Hannah Stanley.
> Activist and educator. From *A Voice from the South*.

I think one of the biggest things in my life was the time I sang at the Metropolitan Opera. My mother was in the audience and she came backstage afterward. When I hugged her, she said, "Darling, we must thank the Lord." She was a firm believer in the good things that came from above.

> —MARIAN ANDERSON, daughter of Annie Anderson.
> Opera diva. From *I Dream a World*.

The one I really liked best, though, was my great-grandmother, my grandfather's mother. . . . We used to talk about life. And she used to tell me how it felt to be a slave, to be owned body and soul by a white man who was the father of her children. She couldn't read or write, but she knew the Bible by heart from beginning to end, and she was always ready to tell me a story from the Scriptures.

—BILLIE HOLIDAY, daughter of Sadie Fagan. Singer.
From *Lady Sings the Blues*.

I have problems just like everyone else. Whenever I do, I think about my grandmother and my mother. They were such strong women, who always taught me to place my faith in God and to read the Bible.

I remember when I got married, I stopped reading the Bible. When my mother found out that I had stopped, she told me that one should not stop reading the Bible; there was always something new to learn by reading it. On that day, I started back reading the Bible and have not stopped since.

—ROSA PARKS, daughter of Leona McCauley and
granddaughter of Rose Edwards. Activist. From
Quiet Strength.

"Lorraine, God put you on this earth for a reason. He's going to reveal that reason to you. Just wait. And keep your heart open so you'll see it when He puts it in front of you."

—DR. LORRAINE E. HALE, daughter of Mother Clara
McBride Hale. Pediatrician and director of Hale House.
From *Hale House.*

My mother would sing "The Lonely Jesus," and it would sound so good to me. I'd sing "The Long-leg Jesus" 'cause I didn't know. I never got it different until I got to be a big girl. When I was little, I'd get up on the table and sing, "There's not a friend like the Long-leg Jesus, no no not one." People laughin' at me singin' that, but I thought they was feelin' good 'cause I was a child.

—WILLIE MAE FORD SMITH, daughter of Mary Williams Ford. The "mother of gospel music." From *I Dream a World.*

My mother always stressed to me the importance of being the best I could be, never giving up, and the necessity of giving something back—the Bible says to whom much is given, much is required. And when you put energy into the universe, it comes back to you a hundred times.

> —TERRIE WILLIAMS, daughter of Marie Williams.
> President of one of America's most successful
> public relations firms, the Terrie Williams Agency,
> and author of *The Personal Touch*.

Never begrudge others for what they have, because you don't know how they got it. Instead, work hard and pray for the things you need, and you will be blessed accordingly.

> —HEATHER EBANKS, daughter of Yvonne Kangolan.
> Owner, Heather's Lingerie, Kingston, Jamaica.

On Saturdays, my sisters and I often sat on our fire escape and giggled at the Jewish neighbors going in and out of the synagogue. Mother punished us when she caught us at it. She was a deeply religious person and would not hear of our making fun of anyone's religion. Other children made fun of us because Mother enforced churchgoing on her daughters—

three times every Sunday. They would chant, "Here come the St. Hill girls!" as Mother, Odessa, Muriel, Selma, and I dressed up and, each carrying a little Bible, walked to 11:00 A.M. services, 2:30 P.M. Bible service, and 7:30 P.M. services at the English Brethren Church. It was a small, Quaker-like sect that Mother belonged to. "You're going to grow up to be good Christians," she would tell us firmly, leading us past our playmates' jeers.

> —SHIRLEY CHISHOLM, daughter of Ruby Seale St. Hill.
> Former congresswoman and first woman to
> run for president of the United States.
> From her autobiography, *Unbought and Unsold.*

*There is a higher power—a spiritual being—
who watches over you and guides you.*

—MARVALENE HUGHES, daughter of Alverta Hall Hughes.
President, California State University, Stanislaus.

In this business, I remind Whitney that they build you up to tear you down. I tell her she is never to drink the perfume, just to smell it. Since she was a little girl, I've taught Whitney there are two things she can always count on in this life—God and family—and if she's on firm foundation with those, no one can destroy her no matter what.

—CISSY HOUSTON, mother of Whitney Houston.
Singer. From *Ebony*, February 1988.

My mother used to tell me, "If you ever get too big for your britches, just remember who God is. He's bigger than you and bigger than me."

—WHITNEY HOUSTON, daughter of Cissy Houston.
Entertainer. From *Essence*, December 1990.

God and time are synonymous, and through time, God reveals all things—Be patient.

—DIANNE REEVES, daughter of Vada Burrell-Swanson. R&B singer.

My mother gave me something to live on if she weren't around—spirituality and faith. She gave me her base, her spiritual base, her unshakeable base.

—GLADYS KNIGHT, daughter of Elizabeth Knight. Singer. From *Ebony*, May 1992.

My grandmother gave me the gift of prayer and faith as she demonstrated both strongly in my life. She was a dressmaker, earning a living sewing in our rented home. When there were not enough customers to pay our bills, she simply talked to God in her heart as if she were holding a conversation with me. She went to night school at the age of seventy-five to earn a high school diploma. Her faith required action. To this day, my prayers of faith have kept me strong. I shall always be grateful to her. Even now many times she is praying and singing through me!

—DR. BARBARA LEWIS KING, granddaughter of Mrs. Ida Bates Lewis.
Founder-minister of the Hillside Chapel and Truth Center in Atlanta.

Jesus wept.

—NTOZAKE SHANGE, daughter of Eloise O. Williams.
Author of the Obie-winning "choreopoem,"
*for colored girls who have considered
suicide/when the rainbow is enuf*
and many other works.

Where there's a will, there's a way. If you provide the will, God will provide the way.

—BEVERLY BAILEY HARVARD, daughter of Irene Perkins Bailey. Chief of police, the city of Atlanta, and the first African-American female to head a major metropolitan police department.

God gave you a very special talent, so whenever you're in doubt or you fear anything, repeat the 23 Psalms of David and just know that the Lord watches over you.

—JOANNE (B. J.) CROSBY, daughter of Eldora Brooks Crayton. Tony-nominated actor in the Broadway play *Smokey Joe's Cafe.*

Pray to God, and you'll never be alone.

—DENISE CAVITT MATTHEWS, daughter of Malinda Williams Cavitt. Systems manager.

The Lord never gives you too much of a burden. The Lord helps those who help themselves.

—CHERYL NELSON, daughter of Blanche Borden. Systems coordinator.

Raise your children in the fear of the Lord.

—CECE WINANS, daughter of Delores Winans. Singer.
From *Jet*, May 9, 1994.

My mother always encouraged us to keep moving forward with the words: "If you take one step, God will take two."

—CARRIE P. MEEK, daughter of
Carrie Tansy Pittman. Former teacher,
granddaughter of a slave, and a member of
the U.S. Congress, representing Florida's
17th congressional district in Miami (Democrat).

Mother is not here to see my success; however, I am confident in the belief that she is still watching over me, smiling and saying, "Well done, daughter. Mother is proud of you." Each time I kneel to pray, I ask God to say "Hello" to Mother for me because I know she is flying around God's Throne, singing. She loved to sing, although she couldn't carry a tune in a bucket, but I know God is letting her sing . . . *and still, I cry.*

—BARBARA ROBINSON. Activist, business owner, and educator. From *And Still, I Cry.*

Earning a Day's Keep:
The Gift of Work

Ever since we were children, it has been ingrained in our heads that because we were black we'd have to work twice as hard as others to get ahead, but we'd also have to deliver twice as much in order to be recognized. Although we may have moaned about this unfairness, over time we have realized just how true our mothers' words of wisdom were. Our mothers knew that there were always people who automatically assumed we were lazy just because of our skin color. We never could take it easy or let our guard down because we never knew when we would encounter one of these poor, naive fools.

Our mothers practiced what they preached. It seemed as though they worked around the clock to put a roof over our heads, clothes on our backs, and food on the table. Oftentimes, they were forced to work two or three jobs just to make ends meet. That left us, their daughters, taking on many of the household duties. We were forced to learn about responsibility and hard work early in our lives.

Our mothers always assumed that we would work outside of the home. There was never a choice—work was a necessity, not a privilege. We would follow in the footsteps of our grandmothers and great-grandmothers, working our fingers to the bones because "money doesn't grow on trees!"

"Girls," she would say to my sisters and me, "pray as though everything depends on God, but work as though everything depends on you."

—MARY HARRISON, daughter of Jewel Valcina Yearwood. Associate brand manager at Revlon.

I was fired from a job when I was sixteen years old and was devastated. My entire personal worth was laid waste. My mother found me crying in my upstairs room.

"Fired? Fired?" She laughed. "What the hell is that? Nothing. Tomorrow you'll go looking for another job. That's all. . . . Remember, you were looking for a job when you found the one you just lost. So you'll just be looking for a job one more time."

—MAYA ANGELOU, daughter of Vivian Baxter.
Educator and author. From *Wouldn't Take Nothing for My Journey Now.*

My mother told me to be very serious about my work but not to take myself too seriously.

> —DR. SHIRLEY ANN REDD LEWIS, daughter of
> Mrs. Thelma Biggers Redd. First woman
> president, Paine College.

On your way up the ladder, try not to burn bridges.

> —MARVALENE HUGHES, daughter of Alverta Hall Hughes.
> President, California State University, Stanislaus.

Work twice as hard as the white girls when you're in a show, because all eyes are on you.

> —PATRICIA BOLIN, daughter of Sonja Bolin. Fashion model.

Remember, just as beauty is in the eyes of the beholder, so is understanding that the true meaning of success lies in the heart of the beholder.

—BARBARA Y. WHITESIDE, daughter of Blanche Borden.
Administrative assistant.

My mother told me to do my best always, no matter how small the task. She said, "Anything worth doing is worth doing well." She said that laziness is a sin and that hard work builds character. She told me that I should get a good education so that I could stand on my own two feet and not be dependent on anybody. She urged me to let my conscience be my guide and to do what was right instead of what was popular.

She said, "Keep trying to reach your goal. You may stumble many times; you may even fall down. But you don't have to lie there. Get up and try again, and again, and again."

—ANNETTE JONES WHITE, daughter of Delores Berry Jones.
Director, Spelman College Nursery-Kindergarten,
and lecturer and author.

When a job is once begun, never stop until it's done. Be the job large or small, do it right, or not at all. . . .

—CAROL MOSELEY-BRAUN, daughter of Edna Moseley. First African-American woman elected to the U.S. Senate (Illinois, Democrat).

My mom always taught my sisters and me by her actions as well as her words—you do a little more than what is required of you and work a little bit harder than the next person each day.

I have learned so much from my mother. The love and care for me and my sisters was her supreme gift. She went without and sacrificed everything for us. It did not matter to her as long as we had whatever we needed.

—MADELINE K. MELTON, daughter of Pauline Rhodes Kendrick. Sales manager, Chrysler Insurance Corporation.

We children always knew Daddy as the strong and out-front leader, although Mama's entrepreneurial spirit was never far beneath the surface. She always had a dime squirreled away for crisis, ran her own dairy for a while, and was never without an idea about how to manage in a crunch. Daddy could not have kept the church solvent without her fund-raising. When she had to make ends meet and get me and my brother Julian through college after Daddy died, she continued the old folks home and her church fund-raising and organist roles as well as taking in twelve foster children. Like Mama, I have always wanted to earn my own dime.

> —MARIAN WRIGHT EDELMAN, daughter of Maggie Leola Wright. President, Children's Defense League. From *The Measure of Our Success.*

My mother gave me a lecture on collecting salary, and I have followed her advice ever since. She said, "Never start the second week until you've been paid for the first one." She said the law would ask me if the man didn't pay me for the first week why did I do the second. How much law she knows I can't say, but it makes awful good sense, so I've stuck with it.

> —PEARL BAILEY, daughter of Pearlie Mae Bailey. Entertainer. From *The Raw Pearl.*

My mother subscribed to duty. She believed that everyone should do what he or she was supposed to do, and she brought us up correctly.

—GWENDOLYN BROOKS, daughter of Keziah Corinne Wims Brooks. Poet, author. From her autobiography, *Report From Part One.*

One of my mother's favorite mottoes was "Idleness is the devil's workshop." I was to stay busy, to be productive—to do, to learn, to go and be a part of something. "What have you done today to earn the salt in your daily bread?" Mom was forever asking. "Idle people don't sleep well at night. They can't get up in the morning and take advantage of the day and produce something worthwhile."

—DIAHANN CARROLL, daughter of Mabel Johnson. Entertainer. From her autobiography, *Diahann!*

My mother always told me that you should never take this business for granted. You could be famous one day and gone tomorrow. I *always* keep a level head.

> —SHANICE WILSON, daughter of Crystal Wilson.
> Singer. From *Essence,* October 1994.

My mother always taught me to do my best—whether on screen or *off,* whether onstage or not—and to make sure I grew and learned with each new experience and performance. Since my career has taken off, I've found it has been my mother's advice that has anchored me, that has been invaluable to me as both a woman and a performer.

> —JANET JACKSON, daughter of Kathleen Jackson.
> Entertainer. From *Ebony,* February 1988.

I recall my mother telling me that just because you are black, you are going to have to work 100 percent more than everyone else just to be considered equal. That is unfair, but it is the reality of the situation.

> —VANESSA WILLIAMS, daughter of Helen Williams. Entertainer. From *Ebony*, April 1990.

She taught me to care, to dream, and to be prepared to work from dawn until dusk (and beyond) for the things which are important to me. She is a part of all that I do.

> —JESSYE NORMAN, daughter of Janie King Norman. Opera diva. From *Ebony*, May 1993.

You get what you pay for in life, so work hard, stay focused, and be prepared to sacrifice in order to accomplish great things.

—CHERYL K. SERAILE, daughter of Drucilla Brown. Screenwriter.

Don't try to be good; be excellent.

—JANET COLLINS, niece of Aunt Adele. Prima ballerina.
From *I Dream a World.*

Men—The Good, the Bad, the Ugly: The Gift of Good Advice

Our mothers raised us to rely upon ourselves—not on the generosity of strangers, the luck of the numbers, or the sugar from a daddy. This self-reliance was particularly important when it came to men. Under no circumstance were we supposed to rely on men for anything.

It is not surprising that many of us were encouraged by our mothers to pursue educations. Educations that led to fulfilling and prosperous careers in which we could survive financially on our own just in case Mr. Right never came along or we kicked Mr. Right out on his behind.

As their daughters, we've lived through the storms that raged in their hearts. And despite it all, when they found love, they gave all their love to their man. When they lost love, they never gave up the hope of tasting love's sweet nectar again. Our mothers gave us the courage to say "Get out!" *and* to say "I love you!"

As far as my mother was concerned, men were unreliable.

on a man for anything, because if I did I would surely be disappointed. Ironically, the one man I could always rely on was her husband and my stepfather, Charles Townes.

Men are like buses; there's always another one coming.

—BEVERLY GUY-SHEFTALL, daughter of Ernestine Varnado Guy.
Anna Julia Cooper professor of women's studies, Spelman College,
and co-editor of *SAGE: A Scholarly Journal on Black Women.*

Don't love a man more than you love yourself.

—PAMELA JOHNSON, daughter of Joyce Johnson, Ph.D.
Senior editor, *Essence.*

"There is always something left to love. And if you ain't learned that you ain't learned nothing. Have you cried for that boy today? I don't mean for yourself and for the family 'cause we lost the money. I mean for him; what he been through and what it done to him. Child, when do you think is the time to love somebody the most; when they done good and made things easy for everybody? That ain't the time at all. It's when he's at his lowest and can't believe in hisself 'cause the world done whipped him so. When you starts measuring somebody—measure him right, child. Measure him right. Make sure you done taken into account what hills and valleys he come through before he got to wherever he is."

—MAMA, from the play *A Raisin in the Sun*,
by Lorraine Hansberry, daughter of
Nannie Perry Hansberry.

My mother has consistently shared valuable gems of knowledge and directives to help me steer the currents of life. However, there is one thing I recall vividly her telling me which has helped me to age gracefully and with anticipation—"sex gets better after forty." She was right!

> —DYANA WILLIAMS, daughter of Professor Nancy Vives Neuman. President of the International Association of African-American Music.

Always be in a position to support yourself, and if you've done all that you can and he is still not treating you right, leave him. Forget couples therapy, crying to your friends, or feeling sorry for yourself. Simply pack up your clothes and leave.

> —ANITA DOREEN DIGGS, daughter of Gladys Haigler-Smith. Author of *Talking Drums* and *Success at Work*.

In any relationship, mutual respect is of the essence, and if you loose it, your relationship should be over.

> —PATRICIA BOLIN, daughter of Sonja Bolin. Fashion model.

Always let a man know you want him—not need him. And if you want a husband, just set your mind to it.

—NTOZAKE SHANGE, daughter of Eloise O. Williams. Author of the Obie-winning "choreopoem," *for colored girls who have considered suicide/when the rainbow is enuf* and many other works.

The best advice my mother gave me was based on her own life experience: "If I had my life to live over again, I would check out my husband's pension plan."

—BERNICE THOMAS, daughter of Betty Thomas. Owner, Your Hair Salon, Cambridge, MA.

Make it a habit to keep yourself looking good—be prepared.

—CHERYL K. SERAILE, daughter of Drucilla Brown. Screenwriter.

Iman, you don't have to lie down with a dog. You have a choice; you don't have to do anything you don't want to do. One good woman is far better than ten men.

—IMAN. Fashion model. From *Glamour*, September 1989.

Nothing is more infuriating than when a daughter and mother are going at it, and the dad steps in. He'll say to the wife, "Honey, why don't you try to get along with her, understand her?" The wife could strangle her husband for that. There he stands (she feels), reprimanding her in front of the child, as if *she* (the mother) is a child. Now the battle turns between the husband and wife, as the daughter saunters out, head held up, the "victor," it seems.

Once the daughter finds a boyfriend, however—especially one she can twist around her finger—Papa is out. Now it's Mama who's the "highlight of her life." And when she experiences "love problems," she pleads: "Mom, what's wrong with men?" Honey, now that you have one—you figure it out.

—PEARL BAILEY, daughter of Pearlie Mae Bailey.
Entertainer. From *Between You and Me*.

Corine advised her only daughter to be self-sufficient, not to marry early, and to find a man who would encourage her to pursue her own individual interests. With this in mind, she would greet all of her daughter's suitors at the door with a lecture (sometimes lasting an hour) on the importance of education before romance, and religion above all.

> —CAROLE and NORMA JEAN DARDEN, granddaughters
> of Corine Johnson Sampson. From their cookbook
> *Spoonbread and Strawberry Wine.*

She always said to me, "If a man hits you, you get out as fast as you can. You leave smoke."

> —HALLE BERRY, daughter of Judith Berry.
> Actor. From *Ebony,* April 1993.

"We're leaving your father." This was a statement I had spent much of my childhood dreading, waiting to hear, watching it take shape in the bickering, the sniping, and the increasing absence of affection.

That day my mother taught me that you *can* leave: It is never too late to do that. . . . So when I had to, I could leave a man when it was over because I had witnessed my mother saying good-bye to my father when nothing was left.

—MARITA GOLDEN, daughter of Beatrice Lee Reid. Author. From *Wild Women Don't Wear No Blues: Black Women Writers* on *Love.*

She was a sensuous woman who talked openly and vividly about passion and sex, subjects most parents avoided. Sex could be thrilling, we learned from Mama, but "not in the back of a car and not before marriage." She believed in romance and the excitement of young love, but "loving someone and being a fool are two different things."

—GLORIA WADE-GAYLES, daughter of Bertha Wade. Author. From "Connected to Mama's Spirit," *Double Stitch*, 1993.

When the women's lib movement came about, we were all very anxious to hear grandmama's views on *that* subject. She gathered her granddaughters around her. She said, "Generations and generations of Woodard women have always had . . . the opportunity . . . to work like a man, and at a man's job. Oh, we have all worked in the fields, chopped wood, driven trucks, and tractors, and buses. I myself, I worked on the railroad during the war. A woman must always be prepared to do whatever she has to do, for the sake of her family and her loved ones. . . . But if any of you should find a nice young man . . . he comes walking down the street, and this young man just happens to be offering you . . . a pedestal . . . I want you to climb up on it, and take a nap for me!"

—CHARLAYNE WOODARD, granddaughter of Grace Harris.
Author. From her award-winning one-woman play, *Pretty Fire*.

Make sure you marry for love, girl, 'cause money and looks can be very temporary.

—ALFRE WOODARD, daughter of Constance
Roberson Woodard. Actor.

This is how to love a man, and if this doesn't work there are other ways, and if they don't work don't feel too bad about giving up.

—JAMAICA KINCAID, daughter of Annie Richardson.
Author. From "Girl."

*Oh, Mama was a smart woman. It takes
a smart woman to fall in love with
a good man.*

—BESSIE DELANY, daughter of Nanny Logan Delany. Dentist.
From *Having Our Say.*

We Shall Overcome:
The Gift of Strength

It's a sad fact of our lives: many of us were exposed to racism at a very young age—thrusting us out of our mothers' wombs of warmth and security and into an unprotected, cold world burdened with ignorance, jealousy, and hatred. As hard as our mothers tried, it was impossible for them to continuously shelter us from this hostile world.

How many times can you recall as a child being blatantly followed by a clerk in the neighborhood five-and-dime store? What about all those times when some white kid surreptitiously mumbled a racial slur under his breath as you meandered your way through those crowded hallways in high school? Do you recall how some teachers encouraged you to pursue a trade where you could utilize your hands rather than your brain because a physics or trig class was just a "waste" of your talents?

Whether it was overt or covert, we all experienced racism in one form or another. Ironically, there was a silver lining in this storm cloud. As author Annette Jones White writes: "By introducing me to books and the *Pittsburgh Courier*, my mother opened up a whole new world to me, part good, part bad. The horrors of racism and lynchings were bad, but the closeness they generated in the black community was good."

In part, African-Americans have been united because we are the recipients of one of the lowest common denominators known to humanity: *racism*. When this is multiplied by sexism, one cannot help but marvel at all that our mothers have accomplished! And as the daughters of strong, proud African-American women there is no question, we shall overcome!

The first severe reality? When I left Detroit to go to college in the South, my mother was at the train station. She was trying to mumble something. Whatever she was trying to tell me, she was not very good at it, and I laughed to myself. She was a bundle of confidence, and here she was just tripping over her words. But the minute I got off that train, I knew what she was trying to say. She was trying to tell me in ten words or less about racism.

—BETTY SHABAZZ. Activist. From *I Dream a World.*

I came home one day after I got beat up by these kids, saying how I hated white people. And my grandmother had this swing on her porch, as many people do in the South. And whenever I had a problem, I would always go to my grandmother, and somehow the problem would get solved. She would get her favorite pop, which was cream soda, and mine, too, and we'd sit in the swing. And there was something about sitting in this swing and swinging back and forth that just sort of calmed me down, with her talking to me. So I came home in a rage this time, saying, "I hate 'em, I hate 'em." And she sat there and started swinging me back and forth until I calmed down, and then she said, in a very soothing voice, "Before you go to bed tonight, I want you to say a prayer for those people." I loved my grandmother so much, but I found myself saying, "Mama, I can't do it." And she said, "Well, you have to, because you cannot carry hate in your heart for anybody, for any man."

She said, "You're a young person, and one day you'll move away from Texas, and you'll find that all people are not like these people here." I thought about it, through several bottles of soda. And finally, she got me to say I would say a prayer before I went to bed.

—ERNESTINE ANDERSON. Jazz singer.
From *I Dream a World*.

My mother stressed being good, better, and the best I could be. She said, "You must be the best one, the smartest, because *they* will not expect it of you." She warned me that white people would expect me to be inferior, even stupid, but I was determined to fool them. I was determined, with Mama's encouragement and faith, to be the best, and I was. I graduated valedictorian of my predominately white high school class in Berkeley, California, and I graduated Phi Beta Kappa in mathematics from the University of California. Believing that I was better, in fact, carried me through twenty-eight years in corporate America, into academia, and into the world of published authors. I always believed that I could be the best because Mama said it. Not enough mothers tell their daughters that today!

—MARJORIE L. KIMBROUGH, daughter of Louise B. Lindsay. Professor, Clark Atlanta University, and author of *Accept No Limitations, Beyond Limitations,* and *She is Worthy.*

Mama, I thank the Lord for her. She said if you want to go to heaven, you got to love white people. Said God love 'em, He made 'em. That was the hardest thing for me to do, love white people. When I was little I was scared of 'em. We thought white people would just kill ya, do ya mean things just because. Mama kept tellin' us, "I love 'em 'cause they ain't gonna keep me out of heaven."

—PRISCILLA L. WILLIAMS. Mother of fourteen children, although she gave birth to none. From *I Dream a World.*

. . . I knew it was time to stop for a long-needed talk, not merely about race and color but in order to instill the kind of pride in race and in one's self that was part of my up-bringing and of which I have never been ashamed. It was also time to stop the beginnings of prejudice against white people that we as Negroes acquire unconsciously and that I believe is just as egregious as that imposed against us. I told [my daughter] Marion that not all white people are bad, that every person is born with the capacity of loving as well as hating, and that those who hate without cause are blind and ignorant and do not understand why or what they are hating. I told her that as long as people hate each other there will be wars such as we have now in Korea and that people must be taught to love just as they are taught to hate, before the world can be what we want it to be.

—MARGARET WALKER, daughter of Marion Dozier Walker.
Author. From "How I Told My Children about Race."

*My mother believed in freedom and equality
even though we didn't know it for reality
during our life in Alabama.*

—ROSA PARKS, daughter of Leona McCauley. Activist.
From *I Dream a World*.

She tried hard to make her little girl—so full of hatred and confusion—see white people not so much as what they were but in terms of their potential. She did not want me to think of the guns hidden in drawers or the weeping black woman who had come screaming to our door for help, but of a future world of harmony and equality. I didn't know what she was talking about.

—ANGELA DAVIS, daughter of Sallye E. Davis.
Activist and professor. From her book
An Autobiography.

Racism has had a particular sting for African-American women who are mothers, an agony captured in Margaret Burroughs' poem "What Shall I Tell My Children Who Are Black?" As long as we women are the primary caretakers of children more often than not, it is to us that little girls and boys come crying when they are hurt. One of the most profoundly painful emotions in the world is when an African-American mother is confronted with her child's hurt from racism. This experience is inevitable. Even if the child attends an elite preparatory school or lives in a "liberal" neighborhood, that child is going to be hurt by racism. When a child asks, "Mama, what's a nigger?" or says, "Mama, Joanie said her parents told her not to play with me," the pain and frustration a mother experiences is almost indescribable. What should she tell her child who is black? An enormous tribute is owed African-American parents, particularly mothers, who for years have had the responsibility of providing balm for the wounds racism inflicted upon their children and the task of counseling them on how to weave their way through and around its horrors.

—JOHNNETTA B. COLE, daughter of Mary Frances Lewis Betsch. First woman president, Spelman College. From *Conversations*.

*I don't think black or white. I have to tell you
that. I think of human beings. . . . My mother
raised me that way.*

—SARAH VAUGHN, daughter of Ada Vaughn. Jazz singer.
From *Sassy.*

The teacher sat us in alphabetical order, and I was seated
next to a little white girl. My classmate turned to the teacher
and said, "I don't want this nigger sitting next to me." Fortu-
nately, my mother taught me that people who have this kind
of prejudice are blind. Their racism is like a disease that will
destroy them.

—REGINA TAYLOR. Actor. From *Essence*, March 1992.

My mother's careful rearing of me made me see how wrong, unfair, and humiliating it was to have to live in fear that your children might come to harm for just being themselves.

—ANNETTE JONES WHITE, daughter of Delores Berry Jones.
Author. From "Dyad/Triad," *Double Stitch*.

I grew up with the feeling that there were good people and bad people, no matter what color. I remember Mom making that very clear. When anything racist would happen, I could go home to her and she would reestablish the pride in my African heritage.

—JUDITH JAMISON, daughter of Tessie Belle Brown.
Dancer. From her autobiography, *Dancing Spirit*.

In Praise of Mama:
God's Own Gift

They are our miracles, our role models, our goddesses. They kindled the fire of our dreams. They are our moral compasses. They accept us. They love us. They teach us. They reassure us. They reassure us all over again. They protect us. They liberate us. They support us.

The support a mother has for her daughter is like a flame that never fades. There is no stronger or more powerful relationship than that between a mother and daughter. Mothers always kissed our hurts to make us feel better, purchased Girl Scout cookies to help raise money for our troop, practiced spelling words so we would get an A on the test, sewed the most magnificent dress so that we were the queen of the prom, put money in the bank in the hopes of having a nest egg for our college educations, volunteered to take the grandkids so that we might have some peace and quiet. . . .

It's no wonder that within the African-American community we have such a sense of pride and respect for our mothers, because they have sacrificed so much for their little ones, always supporting us every step of the way. Till this day they continue to be our teachers, doctors, ministers, confidants, bankers, protectors, neighbors, best friends— simply put, our angels and saviors. And even though we have grown into adults, as far as our mothers are concerned we're still their babies. And if anyone should dare mess with us, they will have to deal with the wrath of our mothers— what an awful surprise for the uninitiated!

> *To describe my mother would be to write about a hurricane in its perfect power.*
>
> —MAYA ANGELOU, daughter of Vivian Baxter. Educator and author. From *I Know Why the Caged Bird Sings*.

We feel blessed to have had her as our mother. She taught us to live adventurously; to love rain; to suck the nectar from honeysuckle; to make a garden; to fashion dolls from cornsilk; to color Easter eggs with plant dyes; and to recognize birds, flowers, leaves, and trees. She instilled in us a spirit of independence and taught us to stand firm in whatever we thought was right, and to pursue our own dreams until they became realities, without losing sight of the fact that how the struggle is waged is as important as the victory. In the best sense of the word, she was the most "liberated" woman we ever knew.

> —CAROLE and NORMA JEAN DARDEN, daughters of Mamie Jean Sampson Darden. From their cookbook *Spoonbread and Strawberry Wine*.

She sacrificed to give us that which she did not have when she was growing up—leisure, emotional space, and education.

> —GLORIA WADE-GAYLES, daughter of Bertha Wade. Author. From "Connected to Mama's Spirit," *Double Stitch.*

Because I never heard Momma say much about what it was like to work in white people's houses, as a child I had little appreciation for the daily indignities she suffered at work. Despite her years of college training, "day work" was the only option open to her. Had she been white—with her intelligence and education—she would surely have been a highly placed secretary or executive assistant. But the thought of a black woman in a visible, nonmenial position was unimaginable in our southern segregated community. So throughout my childhood, Momma cleaned houses and yearned for a better life. Then one day while I was at college, she called to say that she had been hired at the telephone company. Although I was happy about this new development, I never thought about how long or difficult the road to an office job had been. Now as a woman at midlife, experienced in rejection and disappointment, I understand the courage it took (she was nearly forty years old) to climb this racial mountain. And whenever I am criticized for being stubborn and single-minded, I take a deep breath, think of Momma, and say a silent thank you.

—PATRICIA BELL-SCOTT, daughter of Dorothy Wilbanks.
Editor of *Life Notes: Personal Writings by Contemporary Black Women* and *Double Stitch: Black Women Write about Mothers and Daughters*, and professor, University of Georgia.

My mother gave to me primarily by her example. She was willing to take risks, determined to provide us with opportunities she never had. And she did, as a woman, whatever she needed to do to be able to take care of herself and her children—by any means necessary.

—DR. LENORA FULANI, daughter of Pearl Branch.
Developmental psychologist, activist.

I am most passionate in my relationship with mama. It is with her that I feel loved and sometimes accepted. She is the one person who looks into my heart, sees its needs, and tries to satisfy them. She is also always trying to make me be what she thinks it is best for me to be. She tells me how to do my hair, what clothes to wear. She wants to love and control at the same time. Her love is sustained and deep. Sometimes I feel like a drowning person, saved by the pulling and tugging, saved by the breath of air that is her caring. I want to tell her this, but the gifts we buy on Mother's Day, at Christmas, on birthdays seem only to make a mockery of that love, to suggest that it is something cheap and silly, something that is not needed. I do not want to give these gifts. I do not want to take these times to show my care, times someone else has chosen. She interprets my silence, my last minute effort at a gift, as a sign of the way I am an uncaring girl. The fact that I disappoint her leaves me lying awake at night sobbing, wanting to be a better daughter, a daughter that makes her life brighter, easier. . . .

—BELL HOOKS, daughter of Rosa Bell Oldham Watkins. Author. From "Reflections of a 'Good' Daughter," *Double Stitch.*

Dear Momma . . .

I have to say living out here in the world and hearing a lot of stories about people growing up in their families, thank you for letting me be free. We never discussed choice of profession. We never discussed marriage. We only talked about education. From there you said I could go wherever I wanted. Never did you use my life to fulfill your own agenda, nor did you repeat the emotional violence of your childhood on me, a luxury your parents did not afford you. Every time I ask you about major choices, you just say, "Make sure you're happy." When I ask, "How do I make sure?" you say, "You have to be doing what you're doing to satisfy you and you alone." I'll bet you didn't adopt that philosophy from any feminist manifesto, but from your practical nature. Right, farm girl?

I can't believe how long it's taken me to see you for who you really are. Maybe I can see you now because I'm a woman and independent enough to just stand back and appreciate you. Or it could have to do with the turn of events in life where it's the daughter's turn to take care of the mother. And this daughter realizes how precious her mother is. Part of what makes you so precious is that it seems like there is no way that you could ever be broken. But what makes you divine among God's creatures is that you gave me perfect love as a child, and your love circles around like a force field at this very moment. And I ask myself, in taking care of you will I be half the woman you were to me? Much respect. All my love, your daughter.

—VERONICA WEBB, daughter of Marion Stewart Webb. Fashion model and journalist. From "For Love and Money" *Paper Magazine,* April 1995.

Do you know what it's like to know that you're a funny-looking child but to have a mother who looks at you and tells you that you're beautiful? I was a princess to her. And she told me that.

—SHERYL LEE RALPH, daughter of Ivy Ralph. Actor.
From *Essence*, December 1992.

"My mother died walking along a dusty road on a Sunday morning in New Jersey. The road came up to meet her sinking body in one quick embrace. She spread out like an umbrella and dropped into oblivion before she hit the ground. In that one swift moment all light went out at the age of forty-nine. Her legacy: the blackened knees of the scrubwoman who ransomed her soul so that I might live, who bled like a tomato whenever she fought to survive, who laughed fully when amused—her laughter rising in one huge crescendo—and whose wings soared in dark despair. She asked for little except 'to be' and never preached values to me because of her own example. . . . I carry her with me now like a loose sweater that sucks out the chill on a snowy winter night."

The above quotation is an extract from one of my poems, "Prose Poem: Portrait," that appeared in my volume of poems, *Girl at the Window*. Although my mother has been dead for almost fifty years, she has remained a dominant figure and a guiding light throughout my life. I still write poems about her. She was a strong woman. I am sure that the example she set, despite adversity, and her encouragement and support of me as a developing human being were the prime factors in making me what I am today. She was an uneducated domestic; I have traveled many miles since then. But there is no doubt in my mind that lessons I learned from her made the difference between winning and losing.

—PINKIE GORDON LANE, daughter of Inez Addie West Gordon. Professor emerita, Southern University, former poet laureate of Louisiana, and author.

Momma was home. She was the most totally human, human being that I have ever known; and so very beautiful. She was the lighthouse of her community. Within our home, she was an abundance of love, discipline, fun, affection, strength, tenderness, encouragement, understanding, inspiration, support.

—LEONTYNE PRICE, daughter of Kate Baker Price. Opera diva. From *Ebony*, August 1986.

My mother, who attended a one-room schoolhouse in Woodstock, Alabama, managed through her own perseverance and family support to gain admittance to Tuskegee University, where her professor was the renowned African-American scientist George Washington Carver. She always taught me to have a sense of history as well as a sense of destiny. The spirit of achievement would overtake my thoughts when mother would say, "Baby, you're something on a stick," which meant that I was a special person. Without a doubt I always believed her. She had a knowing about her and a way of presenting information that made her a totally believable woman.

Mother's life journey kept setting my pace higher and higher. To further magnify these high ideals, she would tell me that, "if you can't see it (envision your dreams), you can't have it." As a result, I could always "see" myself moving ahead in life, because mother kept giving me inspiring, personal insights. Although my mama has been dead for more than thirty years, her words, her thoughts, and her profound lessons keep instructing me on the critical issues of life. She wanted to prepare me for all the challenges that I might face as an African-American woman. And she really did.

—DR. GWENDOLYN GOLDSBY GRANT, daughter of Ethel Lee Mixon Goldsby. Psychologist, consultant, advice columnist for *Essence* magazine, and author of *The Best Kind of Loving: A Black Woman's Guide to Finding Intimacy*.

I owe my mother a great deal. She gave so unselfishly of herself and made many sacrifices for me. I hope she is proud of the person I have become.

—ANNETTE JONES WHITE, daughter of Delores Berry Jones. Author. From "Dyad/Triad," *Double Stitch*.

It wasn't so much what she said, the words spun out in long, thick threads, or what she did, underscoring her words with flashing eyes or a sudden twist of the head. No, it was the way she lived that taught me my most important lesson: courage.

One memory stands out. It was 1956 and I had returned home to visit. Mother left early every morning to drive through the streets of Montgomery, picking up women in rundown shoes and men in starched overalls who refused to ride in the back of the bus. One night, the silence was shattered by the sharp ring of the telephone. "Come quick," a friend urged. "Reverend King's house has been bombed!" Mother and I ran out into the January darkness, hurrying toward the little frame house on Jackson Avenue, near where I grew up. We joined a small group of neighbors, solemn and silent, who were standing in the front yard whispering among themselves: "Dr. King is away. . . . Mrs. King is in the back with the baby. . . . The bomb exploded in the front of the house. . . ."

Several policemen stood in the yard facing us. Suddenly, one of them shouted, "Get back. You people, move on away from here," as he began walking ominously toward us, one hand on his holster and the other on his billy club. One by one, we began to retreat toward the sidewalk, but Mother stood her ground. "Didn't you hear me, girl?" he asked. Terrified, I whispered, "Mother, Mother, come here. Please come back." But Mother just stood there. She would not be moved.

—MIRIAM DECOSTA-WILLIS, daughter of Beautine Hubert DeCosta Lee. Professor, University of Maryland, and editor of *The Memphis Diary of Ida B. Wells* and *Erotique Noire*.

Though my mother imparted many words of wisdom to me throughout my life, she really needn't have said such things. It was inevitable that one day I would look back and realize that I am the daughter of a goddess, in every sense of the word. My mother taught me about the value of life—all life—and the importance of recognizing the love that binds us all. Through listening to her stories of her participation in the civil rights movement in Albany, Georgia, or sitting with her by the record player as a young girl and listening to Clarence Carter's "Patches," Native American singer Buffy Sainte-

Marie's "My Country 'Tis of Thy People You're Dying," or reading her books about the Holocaust, I learned the necessity of respecting the differences between people and the joy of seeking out those who offer new ideas and perspectives. Through gazing with appreciation at bunnies on our lawn, helping her to take care of the many stray animals I'd carry home over the years, or helping her nurse baby birds that managed to crash into our windows, I learned that the way humans treat animals is a commentary on how we treat each other. In listening to her always know the right thing to say or do when someone was sick or in trouble or had lost a loved one and understanding why, in times of need, everyone came to her, I learned that I could have no higher aspiration in life than to somehow learn to do as much as she has done for her family and the world, and with the grace with which she has done it.

—SHARMIAN L. WHITE, daughter of Annette Marie
Jones White. Attorney.

It is difficult to describe Mother's purity and simplicity of character, and she will find it embarrassing that I speak of her in print. But I must. A great deal of what I am and what I achieved I owe to her. Not once can I recall, from my earliest recollections, hearing Mother lift her voice to us in anger. Even after father's death, when she was grief stricken and sorely troubled, she was not short with us. When she corrected us she used a conversational tone. She could be firm, and we learned to respect her wishes. She did not use the rod, but she had a strap, a leather affair about twelve inches long that was plaited at the top and that had ends hanging free. If there was need to add weight to her words, Mother would scurry off and bring back the strap. She would wave it in front of us as she talked, and that was nearly always enough.

—MARIAN ANDERSON, daughter of Annie Anderson.
   Opera diva. From her autobiography,
   My Lord, What a Morning.

No lady cookinger than my Mommy
smell that pie
see I don't lie
No lady cookinger than my Mommy.

—MAYA ANGELOU, daughter of Vivian Baxter.
Educator and author. From her poem
"Little Girl Speakings."

Role model? My mother leads the pack. When I think of the price she paid for "this life." I regard her as I do all of the other black women throughout history: miraculous. They are miracles in this human race. Somehow they are always at the bottom of the ladder, the last rung. And somebody is always trampling on their fingers. Yet despite the pain, the bruises and the bleeding, they did not let go. They hung on for as long as they could, and when they felt they had rallied enough strength from within to reach for the next rung, they did. Those are the role models!

—CICELY TYSON, daughter of Theodosia Tyson.
Actor. From *I Dream a World.*

And every night she set aside time to dress my hair—applying the Vaseline, then wrapping each curl in pieces of brown grocery bag paper so that I would have curls just as nice as Shirley Temple's.

It was my mother's way to prepare me for life and, for better or worse, she made me different. She made me feel better and stronger; she made me feel I could do anything. She had her dreams for her little girl, and she was determined to make them come true. For herself. And for me. Mabel, who grew up on Grandma Faulk's farm in Bladenboro, North Carolina, had had to struggle all her young life just to survive; she wanted, like all mothers, the best for her little girl.

—DIAHANN CARROLL, daughter of Mabel Johnson.
Entertainer. From her autobiography, *Diahann!*

When I was very young, I had a recurring nightmare of being pulled into our dark den by unknown hands while my mother peeled vegetables in the kitchen sink. When I opened my mouth to call for her, I was mute. I would wake each night in a sweat, crying for her to come to my room. Each night she came. Finally one night she said to me, "The next time you have the dream and you can't yell for me, take a deep breath, count to three, and then you will be able to speak." On that night she taught me how to control my dreams, and I've been doing it ever since. Because I believed her, I willed myself to scream. She gave me back my voice when I was a child, and later when I became an adult, she gave me her own steady voice through a poem.

Her poem begins, "Dear child of mine whose given name means black," and ends, "I've been in your corner all along." It is still on its original ragged sheet of paper, partially typed and handwritten, and is the possession that I treasure most. I keep it folded in my first journal and read it whenever I need assurance before I leap. Assurance that my support system is intact, unyielding, and unconditional. In fourteen lines she has written that no matter where I go, what I do, success or failure, right or wrong, she will be the base I can come back to with no questions asked. With her words she has given me license to try, confidence to compete, the imagination to wonder, the desire to explore, and the never-ending need to fly.

—MELANIE F. WHITE, daughter of Annette Marie Jones White. Poet.

Life Lessons:
The Gift of Wisdom

Throughout our childhoods, our mothers filled our heads with wisdom about life. Whether by words our mothers uttered or the behavior they exhibited, we were continually learning the difference between right and wrong.

Today as adults, we often catch ourselves reciting the phrases or mimicking the behavior of our mothers, just as they recited the words and mimicked the behavior of their mothers. Sometimes we are overwhelmed with joy to witness our mother's lasting imprint, while other times we are quite surprised and a little scared. Although we may have vowed as children that we would never be as conservative or frugal as our mothers, as adults we're glad we broke those vows. We realize that practically everything our mothers did was in our own best interest, whether it was making us save those pennies we wanted to spend on candy for a rainy day or steering us clear of those boys who only had one thing on their minds.

Yes, with the wisdom that is cultivated only from years of trial and error, I now have a greater appreciation for the life lessons my mother tried to instill in me. Believe it or not, Mom, some of the things you said went in one ear and actually stayed inside of me! And of course you were right when you uttered that universal phrase of all mothers just before you doled out my well-deserved punishments: "One of these days you'll thank me for this." Thank you so much, Mom, for caring enough about my misdeeds to set me straight!

I tell you, my grandmother was our hero! She was afraid of nothing! She would sit us on the front porch and teach us "life lessons." "Never let anybody have the last word if you know you right!"

—CHARLAYNE WOODARD, granddaughter of Grace Harris. Author. From her award-winning one-woman play, *Pretty Fire*.

I'm fortunate to have come from a long line of outspoken women. Around 1905 my great-great-grandmother Madam C. J. Walker (1867–1919) literally had a dream in which she said her secret formula for treating black women's hair was revealed to her by an African man. The fortune she made through her hair-care products business transformed her from a poor washerwoman into one of the first self-made American women millionaires and allowed her to build a factory, create jobs, launch thousands of African-American women into their own businesses, and contribute to numerous educational institutions, civil rights causes, and women's organizations.

Although Madam Walker was long gone by the time I was born, I have discovered many of her letters, speeches, and published quotes. Two of my favorites are as follows:

"The girls and women of our race must not be afraid to take hold of business endeavor and, by patient industry, close economy, determined effort, and close application to business, wring success out of a number of business opportunities that lie at their very doors."

"I got myself a start by giving myself a start. . . . I had to make my own opportunity. . . . That is why I want to say to all [the] women present, 'Don't sit down and wait for opportunities to come. You have to get up and make them!' "

My mother, A'Lelia Mae Perry Bundles (1928–1976), was a businesswoman, the fourth woman in her family to serve as president of the Madam C. J. Walker Manufacturing Company, the first black woman elected to the school board in our local district, a chemistry major in college, could do a mean rendition of "Ballin' the Jack," was known for her annual Memorial Day parties, and remains, twenty years after her death, my favorite woman.

Much of her advice still makes a lot of sense. When I first started dating, in the days when a phone call cost ten cents, she'd remind me, "Always keep a dime so you can call home."

When I was eight or nine and we had our first mother-daughter talk about sex, I asked her how "it" felt. She must have been shocked but didn't let on, and thankfully refused to tell me anything less than the truth. "It feels good, but it's always better with someone you love," she said. And she was very, very right.

After I'd used my baby-sitting money a few times for disastrous fashion selections, she said, "It's better to have a few nice outfits than a whole closet of cheap things. Always keep one good, classic dress so you can go out to dinner."

Once, after she had to set someone straight for a racial slight, she said, "What racism has done in America is give white people a false sense of superiority and black people a false sense of inferiority. Don't buy that! Always look those people in the eye and speak up for yourself!"

She and her friend Minnie Norris both used to say, "Houseguests are like fish. After three days, they stink." At the same time, she also taught me that the way to be a good houseguest who's invited back is to help the hostess. Wash the dishes. Buy some groceries. Take the family out to dinner. Send flowers. And always write a thank-you note.

—A'LELIA PERRY BUNDLES, daughter of A'Lelia Mae Perry Bundles.
Award-winning producer, ABC News, and author of
Madam C. J. Walker: Entrepreneur, a biography of her
great-great-grandmother.

Remember, wherever you are and whatever you do, someone always sees you.

—MARIAN ANDERSON, daughter of Annie Anderson. Opera diva.
From her autobiography, *My Lord, What a Morning*.

My mother told me always to speak up for what you believe in . . . and I've been speaking up ever since! She also instilled in me the belief that we were put on this earth to make an impact and leave things a little better than they were before we entered. And so I delight in trying to make a contribution and giving to others.

—DR. HELENE GAYLE, M.D., daughter of Marietta Gayle.
Director, National Center for HIV, STD, and TB Prevention,
at the Centers for Disease Control and Prevention, Atlanta, GA.

If ain't nobody talkin' about you, you ain't doing nothing.

—ALFRE WOODARD, daughter of Constance Roberson
Woodard. Actor.

Papa and Mama taught us early in life to "bend a little." We carried images in our heads of ourselves breaking in half. Their statement was, "Stand like an oak and bend like a willow." Their reasoning was to teach us the art of "compromise." We try to live that in our marriage, family, and work. The more we practice "standing and bending," the easier life becomes; rough moments become smoother.

—PEARL BAILEY, daughter of Pearlie Mae Bailey.
Entertainer. From *Between You and Me.*

"Don't you ever go around where you don't speak to somebody, because someday that might be the very person who could be in a position to help you." That's something I've always kept in mind.

—ELLA FITZGERALD, daughter of Tempie Fitzgerald.
Singer. From *Ella Fitzgerald.*

Anything you don't know about be thankful of.

—ETTA JAMES, daughter of Dorothy Hawkins. Queen of the blues.

*Remember something always: I want you
to live in the best place you can afford,
eat well, and if there is anything left,
send some to Mama.*

—PEARL BAILEY, daughter of Pearlie Mae Bailey. Entertainer.
From *The Raw Pearl*.

A lady used to pay me five cents to bring twelve buckets of water for her from a well down to the corner so she could wash. My mother didn't want me to take that nickel. If people sent you to the store or to get water, she didn't want you to take money for it. She always said you must learn to share your services.

—SEPTIMA CLARK, daughter of Victoria Warren Anderson Poinsette. Activist. From *Ready from Within: Septima Clark and the Civil Rights Movement.*

Sister, there are people who went to sleep all over the world last night, poor and rich and white and black, but they will never wake again. Sister, those who expected to rise did not, their beds became their cooling boards and their blankets became their winding sheets. And those dead folks would give anything, anything at all for just five minutes of this weather or ten minutes of that plowing that person was grumbling about. So you watch yourself about complaining, Sister. What you're supposed to do when you don't like a thing is change it. If you can't change it, change the way you think about it. Don't complain.

> —MAYA ANGELOU, granddaughter of Annie Henderson. Educator and author. From *Wouldn't Take Nothing for My Journey Now.*

"If it helps just one person, it is worth doing." That's what Mama used to say.

> —SADIE DELANY, daughter of Nanny Logan Delany. Educator. From *Having Our Say.*

My mother is eighty-one years old. Although she never learned to read or write, she, to me, is the wisest and most intelligent person I have ever met. In my travels as one of the Supremes, I have wined and dined with kings, queens, presidents, and celebrities, but none have impressed me more than my mom. Her eyes have always shown love. She has always said to me, "Love and Truth is all there is."

—MARY WILSON, daughter of Johnnie Mae Wilson.
Singer, author, lecturer, and an original Supreme.

A female without women friends is like a fish out of water.

—BEVERLY GUY-SHEFTALL, daughter of Ernestine Varnado Guy.
Anna Julia Cooper professor of women's studies,
Spelman College, and co-editor of *SAGE:*
A Scholarly Journal on Black Women.

"A friend is one who knows all about you and loves you just the same." This worthy comment has helped me through all of my life when tempted to reprimand a friend.

> —KATHERINE DUNHAM, daughter of Fanny June Taylor Dunham. Choreographer and dancer.

". . . Heaps see what a very few know. Heaps start, but a very few go."

> —VANESSA BELL-ARMSTRONG, daughter of Mildred Bell. Gospel singer.

Always keep an open mind if you want to be an independent thinker.

> —AUDREY EDWARDS, daughter of Bertie Edwards. Editor-at-large, *Essence,* and author of *Children of the Dream: The Psychology of Black Success.*

You can always wear the same thing—it's the attitude that changes!

—JUNE C. HORNE, granddaughter of Ruth Gordon.
Senior buyer, Saks Fifth Avenue.

A woman is not fully dressed without her jewelry. It sets the tone, be it sassy or serene.

—SANDRAYVONNE BAKER, daughter of Thelma Baker.
President, Sandy Baker Jewelry.

Girl, don't grow up to be no slovenly woman.

—HERMINE PINSON, granddaughter of Grandma Yetta.
Professor, the College of William and Mary, and poet.

Other than the Lord, my grandmother always insisted that I avoid putting myself in a position to depend on, or become obligated to, anyone. She encouraged me "to develop my own cornerstones of life by exhibiting initiative, imagination, individuality, and most of all, independence."

> —PATRICIA L. FULLARD, granddaughter of Frances V. Tribble.
> Sales manager, Warner/Elektra/Atlantic Records.

My mother has always been very supportive of me in everything that I do. She has said many inspirational things, but the one that stands out in my mind is "it doesn't matter what the person you love looks like; it's the fact that you give love and accept love that matters." Her words have been especially sustaining since I came out as a lesbian.

> —MATTIE RICHARDSON, daughter of Ruthel Richardson.
> Activist and author.

My mother and my paternal grandmother have always been my champions. My grandmother was the living example of joy, humility, service to others and God, and what it means to take pride in who you are and what you do. She always found a way to see the positive in life. She made it look so easy. My mother is a survivor. She's resourceful, smart, and diligent. Yet she always seemed to struggle against the odds. She always maintained a tough demeanor to stay alive, which often left us without hugs or tender kisses, but her love was never in question. She taught me respect, perseverance, and love for the Lord. I'm a better person because of the two of them. . . . "I see the joy in life, but I'm prepared for the fight."

> —DAWNN J. LEWIS, daughter of Joyce Lewis and granddaughter of Olga Browne. Actor and Grammy Award–winning singer, songwriter, producer, and best known for her roles as Jaleesa on *A Different World* and Robin in *Hangin' with Mr. Cooper.*

Because my mom never realized some of her lifelong dreams, because of marriage, she would always say the following things to me: "Whatever makes you happy—do it! If you see something you want and you can afford it—buy it! Don't depend on a man for anything! Life is very short; enjoy it and live it to the fullest!"

> —LaVERNE PERRY, daughter of Nellie Perry.
> Started as a receptionist and worked her
> way up to vice president, Epic Records.

An antidote to criticism: "If the shoe
doesn't fit, don't wear it!"

—BEVERLY GUY-SHEFTALL, daughter of Ernestine Varnado Guy.
Anna Julia Cooper professor of women's studies, Spelman College,
and co-editor of *SAGE: A Scholarly Journal on Black Women*.

Trust not a living soul and walk quietly among the dead.

—DONNA BROOKS LUCAS, daughter of Rachel Couch Brooks.
President, BR&R Communications, one of Chicago's most
successful public relations firms.

My mother told me, "Hope for the best, but be prepared for
the worst. Life is shocking, but you must never appear
shocked. For no matter how bad it is, it could be worse; and
no matter how good it is, it could be better."

—MAYA ANGELOU, daughter of Vivian Baxter.
Educator and author. From *Ebony*, May 1992.

My mother taught my sister and me that we were strong, important people who had as much to offer, if not more, in any endeavor we chose to pursue. I have always been self-confident because of my mother's words of wisdom, from my birth to her death. When others were uncooperative or vindictive, she would say, "The old cow needs its tail more than one time to fan flies." Meaning be patient, be proactive versus reactive. People have to come back to you for some favor, words, et cetera, at a later time. "Know what battle to fight."

—L. CELESTINE GRIMES, daughter of Lovie B. Austin. Principal, P.S. 118, in Queens, New York.

I am always known as different by my peers, because my mother taught me to be original in everything I do . . . speaking, dressing, thinking, being a strong woman. . . .

My mother raised me the best way she knew how and at least hoped I listened, so that I could be independent and not dependent on her. She always said, "What would you do if I was to die tomorrow?"

—BIANCA LA RUE BARNETT, daughter of Willa Bea Barnett.
Fashion model.

Be yourself, and have confidence in yourself.

—WILMA RUDOLPH, daughter of Blanche Rudolph. Three-time
Olympic gold medalist. From the *Chicago Tribune*.

I had heard Momma say if you asked for things, a heap of times it made it harder for you, and I believed more like Momma.

—WILLIE MAE WRIGHT, daughter of Jennie Cartwright,
born "American, Southern, female, and black." Author.
From her autobiography, *Willie Mae*.

My mom tried to teach me two really important things—try not to be so gullible and don't believe everything people tell you. And trust in yourself. I'm still learning on both counts.

—PATTIE LABELLE, daughter of Bertha Holte. Entertainer. From *Ebony*, May 1992.

Live your life to the fullest and experience things on your *own*—not through someone else's experience.

—LEAH M. WILCOX, daughter of Mildred Oliver Wilcox. Vice president, Player & Talent Relations, National Basketball Association.

While my mother's English is limited, she manages to convey everything and lift my spirits. "Nobody is fit to do anything by herself, you need a team of love. . . . Uwa Musi: Love, honor, support begins at home first. . . . Have courage. Be encouraged."

—AKURE WALL, daughter of Margaret Odueki Aboira Wall. Fashion model.

Life gives you back what you put into it—raise your expectations and you can change your life.

> —ELYNOR A. WILLIAMS, daughter of Naomi Williams.
> Vice president, Sara Lee Corporation.

My mother often said, "Take what you have and make what you want." I learned that this applies to talent and aptitude as well as to material things.

> —CAROL D. SMITH SURLES, daughter of Versy Lee Smith.
> President, Texas Woman's University.

"Let the food stop your mouth." Even though I was only eight when my mother first said this to me, I knew she did not have table etiquette on her mind. Mama was telling me in her usual cryptic manner to stop talking long enough to listen to others, to pay attention to how *they* might be experiencing the world. While growing up, I thought of Mama as meek, unwilling to state her position strongly, and therefore passive. What I didn't realize until I gained a bit of maturity and wisdom, was that while all around her others gabbed and seemed to have a good time, Mama observed, contemplated, and understood human nature. Now, people would never describe me as talkative. In fact, I have the reputation of being introspective and observant, and my writing reflects those values. I thank Mama for that long-ago lesson.

—LINDA RAYMOND, daughter of Lillian Robinson.
Author of *Rocking the Babies*.

If you hold your hand closed, nothing can get out, but nothing can get in either.

—MARLA GIBBS, daughter of Ophelia Kemp. Devoted to God and her community, and blessed with the opportunity to contribute through TV's *The Jeffersons* and *227*.

I had the privilege of being raised in a household with both my mother and my grandmother. My grandmother had many sayings she would tell me, the most memorable being "Save the pennies, and the pennies become dollars." This is what she did as a domestic worker. And when I needed help with the down payment for my home, it was my grandmother who had the dollars.

My mother's wisdom has always had a way of creeping behind me and tapping me on the shoulder. It is now that all the things she told me seem to make sense. She would tell me "This too will pass. . . . Be careful of what you ask for; you might get it. . . . Don't criticize people until you walk a mile in their moccasins." But the most profound thought she shared with me was not to let my happiness depend on an-other person or circumstances outside of myself. This I am still learning and trying to practice in my life. In a deeper sense, it's the root of my spiritual self. My mother and my grandmother are what I strive to be . . . queens!

> —TERRI LYNE CARRINGTON, daughter of Judith Anne Carrington
> and granddaughter of Helen Christina Carrington.
> Grammy-nominated artist and a drummer for Al Jarreau,
> Herbie Hancock, and the *Arsenio Hall Show* posse.

My mother warned us: "If you dig a ditch for someone else, the chances are that you will fall into it yourself. . . ."

> —CARRIE P. MEEK, daughter of Carrie Tansy Pittman.
> Former teacher, granddaughter of a slave, and a
> member of the U.S. Congress, representing Florida's
> 17th congressional district in Miami (Democrat).

Momma always felt if you kept your mouth shut, you wouldn't get no flies in it.

>   —WILLIE MAE WRIGHT, daughter of Jennie Cartwright,
>   born "American, Southern, female, and black."
>   From her autobiography, *Willie Mae.*

Feed your enemies out of a long-handled spoon. . . .

>   —CARRIE P. MEEK, daughter of Carrie Tansy Pittman.
>   Former teacher, granddaughter of a slave, and a member of the
>   U.S. Congress, representing Florida's 17th congressional district in
>   Miami (Democrat).

Is she or he paying your rent? Well, then we don't even have to figure in what they got to say, do we?

> —ALFRE WOODARD, daughter of Constance
> Roberson Woodard. Actor.

People who talk a lot are bound to lie sooner or later. You can learn a lot more by listening than talking.

> —DR. MARY L. SMITH, daughter of Byneter Levi.
> President, Kentucky State University.

Mama always said, "Life is good, knock on wood. . . . Remember, you're living history. . . . Don't worry about what other people say. They're just jealous."

> —MARILYN NELSON WANIEK, daughter of Johnnie Mitchell Nelson.
> Professor, poet, and author of *The Homeplace*.

Mama always said, "Always remember these words of wisdom which I am about to impart to you, my dear. . . ." and then she started snoring!

—DORA J. WILKENFELD, daughter of Marilyn Nelson Waniek.
Nine years old and brilliant!

My mother always said things like "Never go into a liquor store unescorted. . . . Always wear clean underwear. . . . Realize you have to work twice as hard as the next kid (and to work is to pray). . . . Read as much as you can, whatever you like. . . . Don't let anyone push you around, ever, ever, ever. . . ."

These lessons have left me a successful businesswoman, wife, and mother with a relatively orderly house, too many clients, an enviable collection of very clean underwear, and a very empty liquor cabinet.

—WANDA FLEMING, daughter of Sylvia Rice Fleming. Founder
and president, Fleming, Sage & Blue, and publisher of *MetroGirls*.

*Love is the only thing we have that never
runs out. . . . You can't empty a cup of love.
The more other people drink from it,
the fuller it is.*

—GLORIA WADE-GAYLES, daughter of Bertha Wade. Author. From
"Connected to Mama's Spirit," *Double Stitch*.

To have a good friend, you have to be a good friend.

—KARA YOUNG, daughter of Rosemarie Young. Fashion model.

Baby, you've got to be smart and independent. But you still
have to be a lady. A lady is not like a man. Don't act like a
man. A man can lie down in the gutter, get up, wipe himself
off, and marry the mayor's daughter. Don't you try that!

People will remember what you did. So be smart, smart enough to be a lady.

—LEE BLISS, granddaughter of Mary Jackson. Senior editor, *Upscale*, and writer-director of *Headphones*, a gospel musical.

My mother always stressed independence, especially for her girls (myself and my sister). As a single mother for the greater part of our lives with her, my mother emphasized the fact that she chose when it was time for her to have children, and it was something done not for the man she was with or societal approval but because it was something *she* wanted. My mother chose to have her children after age thirty, without benefit of marriage, and that was another of her pieces of advice to us as women. Never have a child until *you* are ready, and only if that is your choice.

—KATE FERGUSON, daughter of Mary Ferguson. Editor in chief, *Today's Black Woman*.

"What goes around, comes around." My mother always says to do what I have to do to make myself happy, *but always* take other people's feelings into consideration. It is not necessary to unnecessarily hurt someone else.

—RACHEL STUART BAKER, daughter of Jennifer Stuart. Host on BET's *Caribbean Rhythm*, and former Miss Jamaica Universe.

When it comes to life lessons, my mother always spoke—and continues to speak—through her actions. She travels the world; makes friends wherever she goes (and then they all seem to come visit her back at home); gets involved in her immediate community as well as the global neighborhood; and is a game adventurer through life. At the root of her drive is this simple instruction: "Be curious!"

Through her adventures, she's built a vast network of "family." People call on my mother in emergencies; they also include her in their most precious celebrations. To both, she goes willingly.

—LISE FUNDERBURG, daughter of Marjorie Lievense Funderburg. Journalist and author of *Black, White, Other: Biracial Americans Talk about Race and Identity*.

Always be a sweetie.

—RAVEN-SYMONE, daughter of Lydia Pearman. Actor.
From *Jet*, May 9, 1994.

Nothing is too great to be coupled with the humblest of circumstances.

—VIVIAN ALLEN AYERS, mother of Phylicia Rashad and Debbie Allen.
Pulitzer Prize–nominated author. From *Ebony*, February 1988.

Never cheat yourself by doing "just enough" to get by.

> —CHERYL K. SERAILE, daughter of Drucilla Brown.
> Screenwriter.

Never work just for money or for power. They won't save your soul or build a decent family or help you sleep at night.

> —MARIAN WRIGHT EDELMAN, daughter of Maggie Leola Wright.
> President, Children's Defense League. From *The Measure
> of our Success*.

I thought I could change the world. It took me a hundred years to figure out I can't change the world. I can only change Bessie. And, honey, that ain't easy, either.

> —BESSIE DELANY, daughter of Nanny Logan Delany.
> Dentist. From *Having Our Say*.

Mother always said if you have a problem with someone, you don't hold it inside; you go to that person and work it out, especially if it's a family member.

—JANET JACKSON, daughter of Kathleen Jackson.
Entertainer. From *Essence*, September 1993.

As my mother always taught both Debbie and me, the universe bears no ill to you and you bear no ill to it. And, of course, her best advice, advice to live life by: "Be bold, be beautiful, be free."

—PHYLICIA RASHAD, daughter of Vivian Allen Ayers.
Actor. From *Ebony*, February 1988.

Many words of wisdom came from my mother's mouth, sometimes disguised in the homey and picturesque language of her native South, sometimes couched in cryptic imagery that took me years to figure out. I still haven't found out who Dick was or why his tight hatband was worthy of remembering or why the legendary Parker's mysterious mistaken assumption should be compared to my own mistakes.

Perhaps she had heard her mother repeat these same ex-
pressions and discovered that situations in her own adult
life called them into usefulness.

One saying that I vividly recall, while not seeming particularly profound, was nevertheless a catchy little rhyme. On
various occasions my mother would say, "Fools' names, like
fools' faces, are often seen in public places." Perhaps I had
been denied permission to attend some public function and
was making a last desperate appeal by assuring her that
everybody in the whole wide world was going to be there
and I would be irreparably injured and deprived if I, too,
could not go. Or perhaps one of my brothers or I would indi-
cate how impressed we were by reports of the huge crowds
that witnessed the performance of some popular entertainer
and the amount of applause and money he or she had
received.

Her reply obviously did not mean that only fools made
public appearances and that all the right-minded people
should live in modest seclusion, for my father was a part of a
highly visible profession and, as a minister's wife, she, too,
was frequently called upon to perform public duties. She
was very much at ease in the spotlight and was capable
of making a speech at the drop of a hat. And she did a good
job of grooming us kids to take our places center stage
whenever necessary. Other things were being implied. She

repeated this quotation in many contexts, and through these various situations I began to understand what she was trying to tell me. She was teaching me the distinction between notoriety and renown, between glittering popularity and true worth. Transitory popular acclaim was not as good as lasting achievement; character was more important than reputation. She was instilling in me an understanding that fame with neither substance nor responsibility is unworthy of emulation and that it is more honorable to make worthwhile contributions in the quiet shadows than to make a big splash in the glare of popular approval.

Over and over I have watched various trends burst into and fade out of popularity, and I have seen the careers of various celebrities flourish, knowing that their often undeserved millions were no true measure of greatness. Then I have thought of my mother's wisdom and said to myself, "How true. How true!"

—NAOMI LONG MADGETT, daughter of Maude Selena Hilton Long. Author of eight volumes of poetry including *Remembrances of Spring: Collected Early Poems*, professor emerita, Eastern Michigan University; and publisher, Lotus Press.

My mother, who is my spiritual touchstone,
told me to remember three things in life:
"You have one body, respect it; one mind,
feed it; and one life—enjoy it."

—DES'REE. Singer. From *Essence*, May 1995.

Sprinkle a little pinch of Tide in your greens when you wash
'em. Ooo, I can't stand no gritty greens!

—ALFRE WOODARD, daughter of Constance
Roberson Woodard. Actor.

Enough is enough and too much is foolish.

—VICTORIA ROWELL, daughter of Agatha Catherine Armstead.
Actor and star on *The Young and the Restless*
and *Diagnosis Murder*.

On self-reliance: "Every tub must sit on its own bottom."

—BEVERLY GUY-SHEFTALL, daughter of Ernestine Varnado Guy.
Anna Julia Cooper professor of women's studies, Spelman College,
and co-editor of *SAGE: A Scholarly Journal on Black Women*.

Define yourself for yourself . . . and then share your blessings with others.

—JUDY SMITH, daughter of Evelyne Smith.
Senior vice president, corporate communications, NBC.

Though my mother, the oldest daughter of a Baptist minister and a brick mason, always worked hard, like her family, for whatever she had, and though she encouraged me to do more and be more, her greatest gift to me was being aware of giving thanks for what is important in life, being here. She always said, "Live good *bébé*, it's all we've got."

—MONA LISA SALOY, daughter of Olga Fitch Saloy.
Author, folklorist, and professor, Dillard University.

Acknowledgments

My deepest and sincerest thanks to the wonderful women who responded to my requests to participate in the book by sharing their original tributes to their mothers . . . Terrie Williams, Mary Harrison, Linda A. Hill, Kimberley Hatchett, Nadirah Zakiyyah Sabír, Cheryl Nelson, Madeline K. Melton, Denise Cavitt Matthews, Barbara Y. Whiteside, Cheryl K. Seraile, Bernice Thomas, Wendy Frye, Wanda Fleming, Vivian L. Scott, Heather Ebanks, Renee Williams, Andrea Arceneaux, Barbara Chase-Riboud, Dr. Mary L. Smith, Linda Raymond, Terri Lyne Carrington, Marilyn Nelson Waniek, Dora J. Wilkenfeld, Dr. Andree Nicola McLaughlin, Congresswoman Cynthia McKinney, Congresswoman Carrie P. Meek, Senator Carol Moseley-Braun, Ntozake Shange, Marla Gibbs, Dr. Alexa Canady-Davis, Leslie M. Segar, Dr. Gwendolyn Goldsby Grant, Bianca La Rue Barnett, Marjorie L. Kimbrough, Annette Jones White, Ornetta Barber Dickerson, Marcia Y. Mahan, Pinkie Gordon Lane, Aya, Joyce Carol Thomas, Pamela Johnson, Julia A. Boyd, Susan L.

Taylor, Beverly Bailey Harvard, Elynor A. Williams, Carol D. Surles, Patricia Bolin, Etta James, Dr. Barbara Lewis King, Denise Tichenor, Akure Wall, Veronica Redd Forest, Hazel R. O'Leary, Lillian Lincoln, Eleanor J. Smith, Dr. Rosalyn Terborg-Penn, Anita R. Bunkley, Dr. Margaret T. G. Burroughs, Roshumba Williams, Dr. Shirley Ann Redd Lewis, Kara Young, LaVerne Perry, Sandra Elaine Kitt, Roxie Roker, A'Lelia Perry Bundles, JoAnne (B. J.) Crosby, Leah M. Wilcox, Dawnn J. Lewis, Anita Doreen Diggs, Ci Ci Holloway, Lavada B. Nahon, Donna Brooks Lucas, Beverly Guy-Sheftall, Linda Beatrice Brown, L. Celestine Grimes, Delores Spruell Jackson, Patricia L. Fullard, Mattie Richardson, Sandrayvonne Baker, Regina Nickerson Jones, Dyana Williams, Marion Taylor Hummons, Melanie F. White, Sharmian L. White, Vanessa Bell-Armstrong, Tyra Banks, Mona Lisa Saloy, June C. Horne, Abiola Wendee Abrams, Audrey Edwards, Mary Wilson, Brenda J. Lauderback, Lee Bliss, Kathy Russell, Katherine Dunham, Miriam DeCosta-Willis, Naomi Long Madgett, Rachel Stuart Baker, Tonya Pinkins, Victoria Rowell, Alfre Woodard, Kate Ferguson, Patricia Bell-Scott, Juanita Johnson-Bailey, Lise Funderburg, Dianne Reeves, Sonia Sanchez, Dr. Lenora Fulani, Marvalene Hughes, Hermine Pinson, Dr. Helene Gayle, Veronica Webb, and Judy Smith.

Thank you, Deirdre Mullane, my editor, for your vision, open mind, and hard work. Thank you to all of the good people at Dutton for your enthusiasm. Thank you, Meg Ruley, my literary agent, for your good cheer and belief in this book. Thank you, Scott Matthews, my husband, for your love and support. Thank you, Aunt Daphne, for lovingly raising me as your own child until my mother returned for me.

Thank you to all of the mothers of the women featured in this book for creating my sisters, my inspirations, my role models. These women, your daughters, inspire me to "jump at de sun."

And finally, thank you, Odeline Townes, my mother, for your love, for your respect, and for your sacrifices to make my dreams come true.

About the Author

Tamara Alexandra Nikuradse, daughter of Odeline Townes, is a marketing manager at a consumer goods company. She graduated from Bowdoin College and Harvard Business School. She coauthored eight books with her husband, Scott Matthews, including the national bestsellers *Dear Mom: Thank You for Being Mine* and *Dear Dad: Thank You for Being Mine*. She lives in Boston with her husband and their three cats, Lisa, Black Beauty, and Dog Meat. Although Tamara lives more than three thousand miles away from her mother, she regularly hears her mother's words of wisdom echoing in her mind.

What words of wisdom or advice did your mother share with you to motivate, inspire, or help you realize your dreams?

If you'd like to share your mother's words of wisdom for future editions of this book, please send them to: Tamara Nikuradse, 304 Newbury St., #430, Boston, MA 02115.

Please include your mother's name, your pertinent biographical information, and your address. Thank you!